WINTER

MELON

William Wong Foey

WINTER MELON
Copyright © 2012 by William Wong Foey

Paperback
ISBN 13: 978-1-93763-341-0
ISBN 10: 1-937632-41-5

Library of Congress Control Number: 2012949253

Ebook
ISBN 13: 978-1-93763-229-8
ISBN 10: 1-937632-29-6

Published by Dark Planet Publishing
www.DarkPlanetPublishing.com

Printed in the United States of America

Dedicated to Buddy

Contents

Prologue... v

Chapter 1 1

Chapter 2 6

Chapter 3 14

Chapter 4 24

Chapter 5 32

Chapter 6 43

Chapter 7 48

Chapter 8 57

Chapter 9 62

Chapter 10 71

Chapter 11 78

Chapter 12 85

Chapter 13 89

Chapter 14 99

Chapter 15 103

Chapter 16 109

Chapter 17 118

Chapter 18 126

Chapter 19 135

Chapter 20 141

Chapter 21 147

Chapter 22 155

Chapter 23 163

Chapter 24 169

About the Author 176

Prologue

China in the late 1930s was a world turned upside down. But of course, China being China was seldom upright to begin with. For centuries chaos and suffering had always been synonymous with China.

One particular episode exemplified man's desire and ability to inflict cruelty and sorrow upon other men like no other. This event became known to the world as the Rape of Nanking. To most of the world, this event has become a mere footnote—an insignificant occurrence that foreshadowed a global tragedy that was to begin a brief two years later called World War II.

Chapter 1

The year was 1937. For the Gong family, it began as with most years. The cold, bitter months begrudgingly gave way to mild days, and the blooming flowers in the fields were a dramatic contrast to the bleak gray, white, and ochre colors of winter.

The Gongs eagerly looked forward to the spring planting of their cherished winter melons. The rich, fertile soil of Kiangsu Province nourished the pale, jade-green melons, making them grow large and flavorful.

"It will be a good year for winter melons. I expect a bountiful harvest," proclaimed the proud and prosperous patriarch Gong Chou as he surveyed his expansive furrowed fields.

"Father, even now my mouth waters for the taste of winter melon soup. And of course, mother will toss in a good measure of sweet hung doa," replied the eldest daughter, Ree.

A long line of marching soldiers approached from the distance.

"Hey, sweetheart! You want a good time?" shouted one soldier.

"I am instantly in love. Marry me!" came another soldier's cry.

"Hey, concubine! How much does your pimp charge for you to pleasure me?" yelled yet another voice from the long column of soldiers parading along the dusty dirt road that paralleled the Gongs' farmlands.

"Insolent bastards!" screamed Chou, shaking his fist at the impertinent soldiers. "I will report all of you to your superiors!"

Ree turned away from her father and covered her mouth in an effort to hide her giggling. The tallish seventeen-year-old, having led a protected life on her family farm, actually felt flattered by the attention of the pubescent young men, rather than being offended by it. "Father, who are all those young men marching toward Nanking?" she asked, regaining her composure.

"My first daughter, they are the Generalissimo's brave and virtuous young men who have come here to protect us from a possible Japanese invasion," replied Chou.

"Why would the Japanese want to come here?" asked a puzzled Ree.

"The Japanese people are monsters, dear daughter. They wish to take things that do not belong to them. They want to own the world. They also hate the Chinese because of the invasion of their island country centuries ago, even though it was the Mongols who tried to conquer them, not the Chinese. I suppose to them, Chinese and Mongols are one and the same."

"Father, how can you speak so badly of the Japanese? I have never met one; perhaps they are not so evil as you say. Besides, what would they want with the whole world? It is enough trouble to care for 500 acres of melons," mused Ree.

"Daughter, you are a foolish nui doy," Chou scolded his oldest daughter. "You know nothing of the world beyond Kiangsu Province. You do not understand politics or how evil men can really be. I can only pray Chiang's weak and cowardly soldiers can hold the Japanese army back."

"Forgive me, Father. I am only a foolish nui doy. But a moment ago you proclaimed the Generalissimo's soldiers brave and virtuous—and now you say they are weak and cowardly?" Ree said with a wide grin.

"My dear daughter, your question only further proves

2

that you are a stupid female. To call Chiang's soldiers brave and virtuous is a gross exaggeration. I was merely being sarcastic," Chou explained.

Feeling hurt and dejected by her father's demeaning remarks, Ree walked away, kicking clods of dirt with her bare feet.

"Ree, put your shoes on!" Chou shouted. "Why do you always walk with bare feet, like some lowly peasant girl? If only they had not outlawed bound feet. If you had bound feet like your grandmother, you would not be so disrespectful to me and your mother."

Ree stomped back to the farmhouse at the far end of the field.

Such confrontations between father and daughter had become more and more frequent as Ree grew into her adolescent years. Father Chou stood statue-like, watching his oldest daughter walk away, until the tall, willowy figure became a distant speck, disappearing into the family's two-story Colonial-style home.

Small wisps of wind danced across the flat plain. This land had provided a good life for the Gong family for four generations. Chou bent over and grasped a handful of warm, fertile soil. He held it tightly, as if it were a precious handful of gold dust. As the middle-aged patriarch pondered the future, a thunderous boom rolled across the Gong melon fields. Startled, Chou dropped to his knees and placed his hands over his ears.

"Nationalist soldiers! You worthless, infertile turtle eggs! The newspaper said they would not be firing practice rounds until tomorrow."

Another deafening boom rang across the fields, then another, and another.

Tears ran down Chou's cheeks in a steady stream. Thoughts raced through his mind as he watched the faint artillery smoke rise upon the horizon. *Does the firing of guns foretell the end of the world?* he thought. *What is to become of my family? Ree is so much like me. A pity she is*

3

a worthless female. She has my stubbornness and tenacity—my strength. Why is her brother so impotent and fragile?

Like most Chinese men, Chou considered it unmanly to cry. But the proud farmer was overwhelmed by the unfolding events. He knew that undoubtedly Chiang's men would eventually come for his twenty-seven-year-old—and only—son.

Chou was very much disappointed in his son. Not so much that he was especially bad or cruel, but the root of it all was Jun's distance toward him and his indifference to the family business. In fact, the young man had little interest in anything, with the exception of a dangerous addiction to opium—a secret his father would soon discover.

Such concerns weighed heavily on Chou's mind as he rose to his feet, wiping away the tears from his face. He dared not let his family, nor anyone else, know that he had been crying. "Will my family and I survive the Japanese invasion?" he whispered, glancing one last time at the wisps of artillery smoke miles away.

This marked the first time Chou had known true fear since his father died prematurely from a stroke at age forty-three. Chou was only nineteen at the time, and as a result, he was forced to take on the responsibility of running the family farm far too soon. Chou walked back to the family home in a daze. He was now oblivious to the incessant artillery fire. Dinner would soon be ready. His wife, Zu, had prepared his favorite dish—crispy-skinned duck—in honor of his fiftieth birthday.

Over the next few months, vague reports would filter in from visitors who had witnessed firsthand the Japanese aggressions across the whole of Asia, as well as bits and pieces of growing world conflicts on the radio and in the Nanking newspapers. But for the Gongs, the endless days of arduous farm labor had begun to dull their fears. The winter melons seemed to grow almost visibly larger with each passing day.

Chapter 2

"Granddaughter, it's so hot. You're sweating and coated with dirt. You remind me of a Shanghai whore," commented Grandmother On.

"Mama On, you hobbled all this way out to the field just to tell me I look like a whore, yet you allowed men to disfigure your feet by binding them when you were a child just to satisfy a man's ideal of beauty. So, who is the whore?" Ree replied defiantly.

"So much disrespect, my granddaughter," Grandma On said. "You dishonor me and your family with that sharp tongue of yours. Moreover, my bound feet symbolize my high position in this world. I am proud of them."

"I do love you, Mama On, but life's value should be measured by more than just the shape of a woman's feet. My sister Mi likes to wear fine dresses and look beautiful. She puts heavy makeup on her face. She is a more expensive whore. I walk barefoot on this good land because it makes me feel free, even though I am not. But I can at least pretend that I am free," said Ree.

"My granddaughter, I venture to think you learned to be so outspokenly rude from your gwai lah girlfriend, Sylvia Farnsworth. She has poisoned your mind with Western thoughts. They are white devil thoughts. If I were younger I would..." Mama On stopped abruptly and grimaced in pain as she stared down at her blood-stained, misshapen feet.

Ree rushed to her side. "Mama On, you are bleeding again. Here, lean on my shoulder. I'll walk with you back to the house. By the way, Sylvia is my best friend. She is a good person. Not all lo fons have horns and—"

A bullet exploded a nearby winter melon, spraying grandmother and granddaughter alike with pieces of shattered melon.

"Idiots!" shouted Mama On. "Why do you frighten my granddaughter and I with such a stupid act? Nationalist soldiers have no right to harass civilians in this manner!"

She and Ree held each other closely.

A well-groomed officer with three subordinate soldiers approached the two women. "Dear lady," he said. "My sincerest apology. My men often behave as mischievous children. My corporal will be severely reprimanded once we return to headquarters." His voice sounded rather insincere. "But putting their bad manners aside for the moment, allow me to introduce myself: I am Captain Song of the Chinese Republic Nationalist Army. We have come for a young man named Gong Jun." The captain smiled while removing his hat.

Mama On bristled. "For what reason do you seek my grandson?" she demanded.

"Madam, as you perhaps know, the Japanese have arrived on the south China coast and are moving inland. It is only a question of when—not if—our unwelcome visitors reach the provisional capitol of Nanking. Therefore, it is for this pressing reason that we need every able body with a growth dangling between his legs to defend Mother China." He winked at Ree as he inspected her youthful body. "If it were up to me, I would be taking able bodies that do not have such a growth between their legs, as well."

"Fool!" Grandmother On said, swinging her cane at the officer. "Young man, you are a disgrace to your uniform!"

The young officer batted away the feeble blow with his forearm. "Old woman, I did not come here to be a gentleman. Strike me again, you old hag, and I will arrest you and your lovely granddaughter for obstructing a Nationalist soldier's official duties," he said caustically.

"Leave my granddaughter and me alone. It is my opinion that you toy soldiers are a greater threat to Chinese citizens than the Japanese," Mama On replied.

"I will take you to my grandson. Once you have him, please go and leave the rest of the Gongs in peace."

"Mama On! How can you give away my brother so easily?" asked Ree.

"What choice do we have, Granddaughter? Besides, your father is not without influence. Your brother will not serve one day as a soldier. Of that I am sure," Mama On said with confidence.

"Officer," Ree said, "please allow me to show you to my brother. It would be most difficult for my grandmother to climb the stairs."

"Certainly," Captain Song agreed. "One of my men will assist your grandmother back to the house."

Together the soldiers, Ree, and Mama On walked down the rows of ripening melons to the family farmhouse, a quarter-mile distant. Moving slowly, the ancient grandmother warned the soldiers against stepping on the winter melons.

"Miss Gong, judging from the grand house your family lives in, I believe your father is a man of great means," Captain Song said. "Why is it that you work the fields and dress as a common peasant?"

"Captain Song, unlike my brother and sister, I do not choose to waste my days lying about playing mah jong, drinking tea, and other things I do not wish to know. I take great comfort working the good land—to watch my melons grow ripe and full like the breasts of my lo fon girlfriend," Ree retorted. "It was not your business to ask me such a question. You are a very rude and domineering man. You're also stupid to have your collar buttoned on such a warm day."

Captain Song replied apologetically, "Sorry, Miss Gong. I am only following orders. And as for my manners, I am a man of simple stock. It has been a hard year to be a Chinese soldier. Sometimes I take my frustrations out on others. And yes," he added, unbuttoning his tunic, "it is too hot to have my tunic buttoned."

"Captain , I will now ask you a hard question: Can the Generalissimo's Nationalist Army defeat the Japanese invaders?" Ree's question was rhetorical, having already seen the ragtag appearance of the Chinese soldiers.

"The Japanese are well-trained and well-equipped, while we are poorly trained and poorly equipped. Mao's Communist army is far, far away and cannot, or will not, help us save Nanking. My advice to you, young lady, is that you and your family go as far away as possible from Kiangsu Province," Captain Song lectured. "I am certain that underneath all that grime is an attractive young woman. The Japanese soldiers will rape you and I am not certain my men and I can stop them. What is your first name, if I may ask?"

"The name is Ree. You try to shock me with your words of doom. But I am young and strong. I would fight back and kill, if necessary, anyone who would do me or my family harm. And how can we leave, anyway? My grandmother is old with bad feet—a result of sick vanity you men have placed upon her and this land. In addition, this land is all my family has. Unfortunately, we cannot shovel our five hundred acres into a steamer trunk and take it with us."

"Very well, Miss Gong. You stay on your beloved winter melon patch and allow yourself and your family to be raped and butchered. And although I said you are pretty, it makes little difference to the Japanese if you are young and pretty or ugly and old. They are brutal people. They will do things to you and your family that will make rape seem like a distasteful inconvenience." The captain's eyes and voice seemed to reflect concern for the Gongs, as well as disgust over the young woman's obstinate attitude. "As I have said, I am not certain my men and I can prevent the Japanese from harming you. On second thought, I would not care to risk my life and the lives of my men to save someone so foolish as to not want to save themselves."

"Captain Song, you need not worry about me. From the looks of your thin frame, I think you would not be man enough to save anyone. Aside from that, I would not care to have you or anyone else risk their life for mine. I would then owe that person something in return, and I do not like to be indebted to anyone," Ree responded sharply.

The captain shrugged. "Very well, Miss. The Japs enjoy eating such strong-willed women for breakfast."

Approaching the immense house, a lone figure could be observed sitting on the veranda reading a gwai lah newspaper. It was the family patriarch, catching up on the other menacing conflict growing half a world away in Europe.

"Father!" screamed Ree.

Quite surprised, Chou threw the paper to the ground and jumped from his chair. "What is the meaning of this visit by Chiang's finest? Are you the impertinent fools who fired a shot a moment ago? I thought it was a field hand shooting rats. Have you come to my land to inform me that the Japanese invaders have fled in terror after gaining first sight of the awesome Nationalist Army?"

"You are Mr. Gong?" Captain Song said. "I can see now where your daughter gets such a biting tongue. We have come for your son, Jun. He is to serve in defense of our country."

"Outrageous!" Chou said flatly. "My mother Mama On would make a better soldier. You cannot have him. I am an important figure in Kiangsu Province. I will speak to the Generalissimo about this. He will have your testicles, my tin soldier."

The patriarch felt the hard blow of the captain's fist against the side of his head. Falling backward, his head struck the wooden porch, momentarily knocking Chou unconscious.

"I am an officer of the Generalissimo's Nationalist Army!" Captain Song bellowed. "My men and I are here to carry out an official duty. My leader may very well have my family jewels, but in the meantime I will do my duty—without the interference of some arrogant gentleman farmer."

"You spineless snakes!" Ree cried, cradling her father's bleeding head against her breast. "You and the other Nationalist thugs are a greater threat to us than the Japanese!"

Captain Song's eyes gazed to one side. He felt shame for his violent outburst. He knew he had overreacted trying to prove his mettle to his men. With no reply to Ree's words, Song and his men marched past Ree and the fallen patriarch, and proceeded up the staircase. The sound of doors being forcefully opened resonated throughout the two-story farmhouse.

"You need not damage any more of my father's doors. I am here. The door is unlocked," came a faint voice emanating from the third door to the left.

Stealthily, the soldiers approached the bedroom door.

"Open the door," commanded Song to a subordinate.

Hesitant, the soldier did as ordered. Slowly the hand-carved oak door swung open to reveal a dark, morose, and unkempt bedroom.

At first the bedroom appeared vacant. Only a sliver of sunlight punctuated the darkness. Peering through the thin slit in the drawn curtains, Song could make out a swaying figure on the balcony. Quickly drawing back the heavy curtains, Song and his men were astonished to see a nude young man smoking opium from a long-stemmed pipe, rocking rhythmically to and fro on a rocking chair. "Good day, gentlemen. What can I do for you?" inquired Jun with a sardonic and glazed look.

"Gong Jun, I am Captain Song Tai of the Nationalist Chinese Army. You are a son of China, and all of her sons must rise up to protect her in her hour of need," said a sanctimonious Song.

Rising up from the rocking chair, Jun drew another deep breath of opium smoke. Smiling enigmatically, he blew the potent-smelling smoke into the captain's stern face. "I do not kill people," replied Jun.

"You will learn to kill," spoke an authoritative Song. He struck the lethargic Jun across the face. "Mr. Gong, you will learn to display respect toward Nationalist officers. It is a lesson I have already taught your father."

As Jun sat semi-conscious on the balcony floor, the captain ordered his men to dress the young man. The soldiers half-carried, half-walked the stupored man down the stairs.

Ree continued to hold her father's bleeding head. "You're all disgusting cowards. You have no honor!" she screamed at the captain and his men.

The young captain flung the long-stemmed pipe, striking Ree on the forehead. "Your son will have no further use for this," he grinned.

Ree was not seriously injured. Her dignity suffered more damage than her physical being. Together father and daughter watched helplessly as the soldiers spirited Jun away in a military vehicle that waited in front of the Gong home.

Confused, Chou picked up the long pipe. "It smells of opium. Please, no! My son is an opium addict? Is it not enough that my son is shiftless and cowardly? And now I learn Jun is a drug addict?" lamented Chou. "I no longer care if my son dies by the hands of the Japanese invaders," Chou stated firmly, rolling the pipe between his fingers. "He is not my son."

"You do not mean that, Father! Jun is your son. He is an imperfect man in an imperfect world. But he is my brother and your son," Ree said in defense of her brother.

The patriarch eyed his oldest daughter with a reflective gaze. "And some are so much more imperfect than others. But you are correct, my dear daughter, he is my son—my only son. A son carries the family name while a daughter only carries the family name until she marries. Female children are so less significant than even a worthless son. Yes, I must save him," Chou conceded.

Ree responded with a frustrated grin. "My apologies, dear Father, for not being born with a penis between my legs. I have been trying to grow one for you since I was born," Ree said, her voice full of sarcasm. "Tomorrow, my number-one daughter, we will go to Nanking to speak to the Generalissimo. I think he is a reasonable and good man. He will release Jun from fighting, and the Gong name will not die."

Chapter 3

The next morning Ree rose before the first light of day, as she did every morning. But today she was not to work the melon fields as she normally did. With luck, father and daughter would gain an audience with the savior of China, as many Chinese perceived him to be.

Preparing for such an auspicious meeting, Ree drew a hot bath and scrubbed the dirt and grime from her body until her skin was nearly raw. With assistance from her mother, Zu, she applied makeup and put on a fine dress. It would be the first time Ree had worn the dress since her aunt's funeral, four years earlier.

Before pulling the dress over her body, Ree stood naked before the full-length mirror, something she also infrequently did. Ree did not recognize the woman staring back at her. She was now a strikingly beautiful young woman. Though far from ugly sans makeup and washing, Ree had always hidden and neglected her feminine attractiveness, a result of her resentment that females in China were treated as second-class people.

"Why must China—and probably much of the world—lavish all their respect and attention to the male population?" reflected Ree. "Why was I born with a hole between my legs? How unfair it is."

"Ree!" called Chou. "Stop dawdling. We must leave for Nanking. It may take a good while to meet with the Generalissimo. He is a busy man."

Hastily, Ree pulled the brightly colored flower print dress over her slender body and stormed down the staircase.

"Daughter, you might wish to wear shoes when you meet China's leader. It may not be proper to meet such a great man barefoot," Chou joked.

"Yes, Father," said Ree, glancing at her bare feet and embarrassed that she had forgotten to put on shoes in her haste to get ready. She raced back up the stairs to retrieve them.

Waiting in front of the Gong home sat a finely polished black gwai lah Packard. Its gleaming metal contrasted sharply with the bicycles and mules most locals used for transportation. Chou's newly purchased gwai lah automobile was his most cherished possession. Few residents of Nanking, save the Generalissimo himself, could afford such a luxury item.

Together, father and daughter sped away with the well-wishes of Ree's mother and younger sister, Mi.

Driving the thirty miles to Nanking, father and daughter spoke few words to each other; not an uncommon occurrence considering that they seldom exchanged casual conversation. Of course, there were the odd occasions when father and daughter would stand with pride watching their winter melons ripen and Chou would speak a few kind words to his eldest daughter. But more often Chou's infrequent words to his daughters were of criticism or ridicule.

As Ree eyed the passing countryside with indifference, she began to contemplate her father's distance toward her and her kid sister, Mi. She wondered—did her father ever feel any pride or love for his two daughters?

"Ree! Ree!" Chou spoke loudly with irritation at his daughter's lack of response.

"Sorry, Father. It is not often that I ride in the family car. I was distracted by the beauty of the Yangtze River and the good farmland passing before us," Ree replied.

"My daughter, we will soon approach Nanking. Before we arrive at the Generalissimo's headquarters, I want to say how much I appreciate you coming on this journey to support me in my fight to free your brother from military duty. Your grandmother regrettably is growing very old, and your mother, though a very good woman, is like a timid little mouse. I trust you alone to advise Jun when he inherits my land and possessions. Please advise him well."

Why should Jun inherit all of our father's wealth, being that his only virtue is that he was born a man? thought Ree.

"Thank you for your trust in me, Father," said Ree half-heartedly.

Nearing the city proper, Ree could see with increasing clarity the ancient wall built ages ago to protect Nanking against invaders. Though now obsolete in the twentieth century, Ree and her sister had always been in awe of the high brick wall which ringed the city.

While passing underneath the wall, father and daughter felt a bit overwhelmed by the hectic activities of the metropolitan city—a sharp contrast to the quiet, rural existence the two of them knew on the Gong farm, only thirty miles distant.

Edging along the busy primary boulevard, Chou and Ree at long last pulled to the front of the city's civic hall, the provisional capitol building of China and the headquarters of the nation's leader, Chiang Kai-shek.

A dozen soldiers quickly surrounded the gleaming black gwai lah automobile.

"State your purpose for being here," commanded a uniformed soldier, barely in his twenties.

"Young man, it is essential that my daughter and I speak to the Generalissimo. My name is Gong Chou. I am the largest winter melon farmer in Kiangsu Province. My grandfather was once governor of Kiangsu Province," stated Chou proudly.

"I do not care if your grandfather was emperor of China," replied the young soldier. "No one can see the

Generalissimo without an appointment."

"I demand to see the Generalissimo!" ordered Chou. "It is of the utmost importance that I see him."

"Father, perhaps we should make an appointment and—"

"The fighting could begin any day," Chou interrupted. "Jun may be killed in the meantime while we wait to go through channels to see the Generalissimo."

He got out of the car. Ree did the same.

"Leave now, or I will arrest you and your daughter," threatened the soldier.

For a moment Chou contemplated his options until his thoughts were broken by the outcry of hundreds of cheering voices and applause.

"What is all the commotion?" asked Ree.

"It is Madam Chiang, making her weekly visit to the Generalissimo. The people of Nanking have come out to greet her," the soldier said. "Pay no attention to it. I am not asking you, I am telling the two of you to leave— now!" He shouted so loudly that he could be heard over the roar of the crowd.

As the soldiers began to physically push Chou and Ree into the Packard, Ree impulsively brushed their hands aside and sprinted toward the nebulous crowd of Nanking citizenry.

"Young woman, stop! I will fire!" screamed the lead soldier, drawing his pistol and pointing in the direction of the fleeing girl. Fearing a stray bullet would strike one of the bystanders, the soldier holstered his gun and ordered his fellow soldiers to pursue Ree.

Fighting her way through the swelling mass of people, Ree could make out the image of a short, frumpy woman, conservatively dressed in black. She was perhaps forty, and was standing on the civic hall's steps, waving and smiling broadly to the adoring crowd.

"Madam Chiang! Madam Chiang!" Ree shouted,

waving her arms frantically.

But the wall of noise proved too much of a barrier for Ree to be heard by the First Lady of China.

Inching forward, Ree came within a few steps below the matronly woman, who responded with great delight to the adoring crowd. Now almost within reach of Madam Chiang, Ree again began to flail her arms wildly and shrieked, "Madam Chiang!" in hopes of being noticed.

Ree felt a sudden sharp sting on the back of her head. Barely conscious, she fell onto the hard granite steps. As she sprawled on the steps, more stinging blows from the soldiers' rifle butts struck her prostrate body.

"Stop striking that woman at once! I order you to stop!" Madam Chiang ordered. She was quite accustomed to giving orders. "If you do not, you will answer to my husband, the Generalissimo!"

"A thousand apologies, Madam Chiang," the lead soldier said. "This young woman and her father demanded to speak with the Generalissimo without going through proper channels. They refused to leave the area. When the young lady ran in your direction, Madam Chiang, I feared for your safety."

"This girl cannot be more than sixteen or seventeen and she is unarmed," Madam Chiang replied sharply. "Soldier, I may only be a petite, fragile woman to you, but I believe I can survive the zealousness of a teenage girl. Pick this young woman up off the steps and bring her and her father to my husband's private suite. I will have my personal physician attend to her wounds. I will let the Generalissimo decide if they are worth an audience with him."

"But...but...Madam...I..." begged the lead soldier.

"Silence! Anyone who would risk their life to see my husband should be granted at least a few moments with him. Furthermore, soldier, we do not beat young girls. She is a daughter of China," scolded Madam Chiang.

Embarrassed, the reprimanded soldiers escorted Chou and Ree to the Generalissimo's private quarters. The entire top floor of the building had been renovated from civic offices to a grand penthouse to accommodate Chiang Kai-shek and Madam Chiang, who visited the Generalissimo on occasion. The elevator doors opened to a long hallway.

"Father, this hallway is as long as our biggest field from end to end, and the rock floor is as shiny as our duck pond on a windless day."

"The floor is marble, daughter," Chou said, knowing his inquisitive daughter was probably wondering what it was made of.

"But it's not white like the outside of the building, more like the soft orange of the roses in our garden," stated Ree.

"Marble comes in many colors, and if there is no particular color created by God, man will simply dye it as he so wishes, my daughter," Chou said.

"Move along," snapped one of the escort soldiers. "The Generalissimo is a busy man."

Ree removed her shoes to walk barefoot on the cool marble. "I want the soles of my feet to feel the cool, smooth, beautiful floor. To scratch something so wonderful with my old shoes would be a crime," Ree explained to her father, who looked at her with disapproval.

The walls were adorned with paintings of past emperors of China, and the works of well-known gwai lah artists.

"What crap is this?" queried Chou, gawking at a brightly colored painting.

"Father, it is a painting by the great gwai lah artist van Gogh. They call it Impressionism. Sylvia showed me pictures of such artists in a book," said Ree.

"A field hand could paint a better picture," Chou commented, shaking his head.

At the end of the hall two ornately carved mahogany doors swung open to reveal the Generalissimo's penthouse.

"It's so big, Father," said Ree, staring in awe at the French antique furniture, black marble floor, and the idealized life-size paintings of the Generalissimo and his wife.

In her haste, Ree fell to the floor, trying to put her shoes back on her feet as a side door opened.

"Young lady, you need not worry about covering your bare feet. I work for the common people of China, as well as the wealthy. Though, I've heard your family is not exactly poor," chuckled a tall, rail-thin man dressed in a finely tailored military uniform adorned with medals. "Good morning. Mr. Gong and your lovely daughter, I presume," the man said. "I am Generalissimo Chiang Kai-shek, the supreme leader of China."

"Generalissimo, such an honor to meet such a great man," Chou said, bowing his head humbly. "I beg a few minutes of your precious time. It concerns the conscription of my son, Jun, into your Nationalist Army."

"Certainly I am never too busy to speak to one of Kiangsu's most prominent citizens," the Generalissimo said. "Oh dear! Your daughter is injured. I had forgotten. Mrs. Chiang just informed me of the horrible treatment of my men toward the two of you. My own personal physician will be here shortly to treat your daughter's injuries. And let me assure you, the soldiers responsible for this atrocity will be severely punished." The Generalissimo was very apologetic and seemed very concerned.

Nervously, Ree stood up with her left shoe in her hand. "Sir, it is not necessary for your doctor to care for my wounds, for they are not serious," Ree declared in a cutting tone. "Your men hit like little girls."

The Generalissimo laughed. "My dear young woman, what a pity you are not a man! You would have made a fine soldier," he said, amused.

"I am so sorry, Generalissimo," Chou said, embarrassed. "My oldest daughter has always been cursed with a sharp tongue. It is probably my fault that Ree was not taught better manners."

"Never mind. It is of no importance what women think or say. They're merely lost children that need the direction of men. So, you want your son back?" finished the Generalissimo, quickly coming to the point.

"Yes, honorable sir, my son Jun is the only living male that can carry on the Gong name. Please, please release my son from military obligation," begged Chou.

"China is bleeding," said the Generalissimo. "If she continues to bleed, she will die a tragic death. Think of the young men of China as the bandage that will stop China's bleeding. In fact, my own sons—"

"Mr. Generalissimo, my brother would make a very porous bandage," Ree interrupted. "Dear, revered leader of China, from the appearance of your furniture, you yourself have bled little for your beloved country."

"Such impertinence! If I did not know better, I would think you were a relative of my bitter rival and enemy, Mao Zedong! Miss Gong, I have bled more than you will ever know. I, along with Dr. Sun Yat-sen, drove the Manchus from power to make China a free nation. I have fought the communist cancer plaguing China, and now I must fight the demon Japanese invaders. I am China! And China is me! If China bleeds, I also bleed. So do not be so presumptuous, young lady, to say that I have not bled for China. I have bled buckets to save China." The Generalissimo paused, then chuckled. "Why am I even defending my record toward a lowly woman? And a very young one, at that?"

He turned to gaze out the window at the view of the bustling city below. Chiang's face appeared to be in deep thought. Then, a barely discernable smile came over the leader's face. "Perhaps China can survive without one of

21

her native sons. She has survived three thousand years without the aid of a man named Gong Jun. I will have the poor young men of China bleed for her instead."

"My eternal gratitude, Generalissimo," said Chou.

The much taller Generalissimo clasped Chou's hands and squeezed them firmly in a gesture of friendship. "Incidentally, Mr. Gong, you will kindly donate half of this year's winter melon harvest to my very hungry army. Madam Chiang herself is quite fond of winter melon soup on blustery winter days."

Chou was dumbfounded. "You can't be serious..."

"Your divine daughter asks me to bleed for China; surely you can sacrifice a few of your tasty melons," Chiang said snidely. "Of course, I could ask for all of your melons, but I am not greedy and desire everything, like the Japanese. Good day, Mr. Gong. Miss Gong."

With his demand still hanging in the air, the Generalissimo snapped his fingers, calling for an aide to escort Chou and Ree out of the building. As father and daughter left Chiang's suite, Ree shot a defiant look at China's prideful leader. In return, the Generalissimo fixed his eyes toward the ceiling in total indifference.

"Your big mouth will someday be the death of us all, my daughter," Chou said as the two of them drove back to the Gong farm.

"Your Generalissimo is a pompous donkey, Father. Were it not for Jun, he would have found some excuse to steal our melons—with or without my big mouth. Now you have your precious son and the Gong name will live on," Ree replied tartly.

The patriarch rolled his eyes in frustration, turned the car radio on, and set the volume on high to drown out his daughter's criticisms.

When they reached the farm, Ree wasted no time dashing up the wide oak-wood staircase to her bedroom to remove her dress and shoes and replace them with khaki shorts and a rumpled work shirt. Clambering back down the stairs with bare feet and openly displaying her long, tanned, muscular legs, Ree dashed past her disapproving father and mother.

"Such immodesty. My daughter has too much Manchu blood in her," commented Mother Zu, watching her daughter return to the fields to care for the winter melons she loved so dearly.

Chapter 4

Near dinnertime a dull-green military automobile rolled to a stop in front of the Gong house. Inside sat three soldiers and Gong Jun. As promised by the Generalissimo, Chou Gong's only son was returned, free of any military obligation. The weary but otherwise unharmed Jun was greeted with warm hugs from family members and servants alike. Accompanying Jun was Captain Song.

"Mr. Gong, you were true to your words. Your influence has set your son free from defending China. And as an added bonus, the Generalissimo, in his divine wisdom, has demoted me to the rank of lieutenant," Song said.

"Captain—uh, Lieutenant—you have carried out your order to return my brother to us," said a stern Ree. "Now please leave."

Ignoring the young woman's command, Lieutenant Song warmly replied, "Miss Gong, I respectfully request that you drink tea and munch on almond cookies with me."

Ree was stunned by the young officer's trans-formation from an arrogant officer soldier to a polite suitor. "What? You can't be serious."

The young officer grinned in a cordial manner. "I am serious when I speak of tea, and possibly I can muster up some delicious dim sum bows for us to eat," Song said sincerely.

"Why should I?" Ree demanded. "You struck my father, you struck me, and you humiliated us. You're a bastard! I do not drink tea with bastards."

"I was only doing my job. Being a bastard is part of the job description. But I suppose I was a bit harsh in my treatment of you and your family. Give me a chance to make it up to you, Miss Gong—if only in a small way," he said humbly. His eyes sparkled in hope of a positive response.

"Lieutenant, I would rather my daughter dine with the devil than you," Chou said. "Now go! Before I strike you in the same fashion that you struck my daughter and me."

"I will leave. I do not wish to trouble you any further. But before I go, I wish to tell you that I can save your melons. The Generalissimo is a poor bean-counter. I have a close friend who is quartermaster for all the divisions stationed in Kiangsu Province. If I were to speak to him, he could simply write on his ledger that the army took delivery of your precious melons, when in fact they did not. Of course, I would need a token number of your melons to appease my quartermaster friend, and a few for Madam Chiang's soup to prevent the Generalissimo from becoming suspicious," grinned Song slyly.

"No!" Ree responded. "You heard my father. Leave now!" She was too proud to accept assistance from anyone, especially from someone she disliked.

"Huh..." Chou pondered the soldier's words. "Wait a moment, Lieutenant. You are certain you can make it so that I would not have to relinquish half of my melon crop?"

"Most definitely. This I promise you, honorable sir."

Chou turned to Ree. "My daughter, we should be good citizens of China and be able to forgive and forget. Besides, my daughter, you work too hard. You need a break. Go with the captain—uh, lieutenant—and have tea with him."

"But Father, you said but a moment ago that you would rather I dine with the devil," said Ree, confused.

"We do what we must do to survive, my daughter. Drinking tea with a handsome young officer is not too great a price to save my melons," Chou whispered. Then he grew stern. "Go with him!" he ordered.

Reluctantly, Ree entered the lieutenant's car while the young man politely held the door open for her. Speeding away, Song drove with reckless abandon back to Nanking, leaving clouds of dust boiling up behind them.

"If you wish to kill us both, why not place a gun to my head, pull the trigger, then do the same to your head? It would be less messy than a car wreck," Ree sneered.

"Pardon me, Miss Gong. I'm an impatient man," explained the lieutenant, easing his foot off the gas pedal.

The two did not speak again until they reached Nanking.

Arriving at the high wall which encircled the city, Song parked near a series of steep steps which led up to the top of the wall. He ordered his men to walk back to headquarters, then retrieved a picnic basket from the trunk and took hold of Ree's right hand. Together they ascended to the wall's summit.

It had been a long time since Ree stood atop the stone wall. Climbing the steps, she recalled fond memories of when she and her two siblings had played along the wall as children.

"An awesome view," Song said as he poured Ree a cup of hot tea from a thermos bottle. "What a pity it may soon be marred by war." He grinned warmly as he offered the steamy cup to Ree.

To Ree, the young officer was just a younger version of her overbearing father, though secretly she found the man attractive. Gently she took the cup of tea and smiled affectionately at her host. She then brought the hot tea to her lips and allowed a small stream of the liquid to trickle into her mouth. Still smiling, Ree moistened her lips with her tea-soaked tongue. Then, leaning forward to within a few inches of the lieutenant's face, Ree abruptly poured the remaining tea over Song's head.

"Damn!" cried Song as the hot tea singed his scalp. "Why?" he pleaded as he sponged the tea off his limp, wet hair with his handkerchief.

"Why?" Ree said. "Why not? You terrible man—you struck me and my father, and you made fools of us. What did you expect me to do for you, kiss your ass?"

"Yes, maybe my tea anointment was deserved," mused Song. "I am a jackass and a military officer. Excuse me, I just repeated myself."

Ree stared at Song momentarily, puzzled. Then the young woman burst out laughing, recognizing Song's subtle humor. Catching her breath, Ree took hold of Song's lapel and drew the soldier's body firmly against hers. She planted an impassioned kiss upon his mouth.

Taken aback by the young woman's boldness, Song pushed her away. "Bitch! First you pour hot tea over my head, then you kiss me as if it were our wedding day. What is the meaning of this?" exclaimed the confused man.

"I have never been close to a man. I just wanted to know how it felt to kiss one. I once kissed a special friend. She is lo fon. To speak freely, I think I liked kissing her better," Ree mused.

"Sorry to disappoint you, Miss Gong. I'm an ugly, uninteresting man, but I never dreamed I would lose a woman to another woman."

"I never said Sylvia Farnsworth and I were lovers. Like kissing you, it was only out of curiosity. She is my best friend. By the way, you are correct about two things: you are ugly and you are uninteresting."

"Country girl," Song said flatly. "You're supposed to say that I am wrong. I am, in fact, a handsome and fascinating man."

"I do not massage men's egos. I do not massage my father's ego and I certainly will not massage yours," Ree shot back.

"Miss Gong, you're an odd one," Song chuckled. "Most Chinese women try to make men feel good. Sylvia is far kinder and more feminine than you. I have also kissed Sylvia. I too found kissing Sylvia superior to kissing you."

"Go to hell," Ree said abruptly, startled by Song's revelation. "You lie. Sylvia is my best friend. She would have told me about you. The tea is cold. You may now escort me home."

The return trip back to the Gong farm was much a repeat of their drive away from the farm. Neither spoke nor looked at the other, except for the quick, stolen glances Song and Ree made toward each other when the other wasn't watching. The drive home seemed even longer than the journey from the farm. Finally, the dull-colored military car rolled up to the front of the Gong home.

The pair sat nervously in the running car, both uncertain what to say. Ree's parents and younger sister watched intently with snooping eyes between the narrow openings in the drawn shades.

With a halting voice, the young lieutenant finally uttered, "Miss Gong, the day did not go well. Can we meet again? Maybe next time it won't be so painful."

"Lieutenant, you're annoying. Why should I want to see you again?"

"So you can have the pleasure of pouring more hot tea over my head," Song replied.

"That I would enjoy," Ree said as she exited the vehicle. "You know where to find me."

As she walked to the front door, Ree's parents and sister quickly pulled away from the window, hoping Ree didn't notice their spying. Ree stood at the door and watched Song's car disappear down the road, trailing clouds of dust. She then opened the front door to be eagerly greeted by her inquisitive family.

"What did the young man say?" Chou said.

"What did you two do?" blurted Zu.

"Did he kiss you?" added sister Mi. "I hope not. He is not very cute. He has pockmarks on his cheeks. He has stood in the sun too long."

Ree rolled her eyes, overwhelmed by the pressing questions. "His pockmarks are not that noticeable, and yes, I kissed him—but not before I poured tea over his head," she said.

Ree's parents and sister stood stunned at Ree's words.

"I have an idiot for a daughter," cried Chou. "You have cost me half my melon harvest!"

"I think not. I am perhaps an idiot, but Lieutenant Song is an even bigger one. He very much would like to see me again," replied Ree.

Jun appeared at the top of the stairs. "Sister dear, if I must be a soldier because of you I will never forgive you," he said in an irate tone of voice.

"Be silent, my son," Chou screamed. "I'm beginning to think I should have allowed them to make you a soldier. You're a worthless opium addict! In reflection, I'm wondering...how do you afford the opium on the small stipend I pay you to do absolutely nothing?"

"If my grandson is addicted to opium, it is because you drove him to it," said Mama On in Jun's defense. "Like your father, your heart and soul are very far away from your family. I provide my grandson with opium. Sometimes we share the dream smoke together. Together we run to a better place—to a place where I can forget that my feet are deformed and rotting." Mama On spoke with frank revelation.

Chou stood frozen upon hearing his mother's striking disclosure.

"Chou," scolded Zu, "we all knew that our son and your mother smoked opium. Everyone knew except you. You were too absorbed with your winter melons and making money to see anything else that was going on around you."

"How delightful," Chou grumbled. "My own mother and her grandson are drug addicts. I provide everyone under this roof with fine clothes, though my oldest daughter seldom wears them, and good food. What more could I have given you?" He looked at Mama On. "And you, Mama On—your feet are bound because it is a symbol of upper-class status. A symbol that you are above the wretched peasant women who work the fields."

Mama On stiffened. "Chou, my son, I was only a baby sister, and when I was young and beautiful, I was only a decoration clinging to your father's arm. I married him not because I wished it, but because of an arrangement between your father's family and mine. So what if I run away to a private place for a few minutes each day? And so what if my grandson goes there with me?"

Chou studied the pattern in the wood floor with hurt eyes, too astounded to look at or speak further to his mother.

Ree broke the cold silence. "Mama On, all my life you've tried to mold me into a proper lady and walk as you do, with bound feet."

"It was a lie," Mama On replied bitterly. "Bai hoi— stand aside to avoid conflict. That's what my mother and men have told me throughout my life. After so much water under the bridge, I have grown weary of the hypocrisy."

"Stop this nonsense!" Chou lectured. "We're all family. We're all family! We all have our roles. We all have our duty."

"Damn this family," Jun said with a bitter voice. "You think of me as weak and spineless. I am going to return to Nanking and join up with the Nationalist Army. After I kill some Japanese, Father, then will you think of me as a man?"

"Jun, you cannot do this," Chou begged. "The Gong

name must live on."

"The world will continue to rotate with or without Gongs on this planet. I will hitch a ride with one of the military trucks going past the Gong farm. Goodbye."

"Jun, my only son, you cannot do this. The Gong name must live on. It would be foolish for you to risk your life to prove a point!"

The family watched, dumbfounded, as Jun proceeded out the front door.

"What will I do without a son?" said a sorrowful Chou, tears streaking his narrow, smooth-skinned face. "The Gong name must go on."

For the Gong daughters, witnessing their father, the proud patriarch, crying openly in their presence for the first time was as much of a shock as seeing their brother leave to make his own way.

Mama On handed Chou a pipe that she carried in her apron pocket. "Smoke this, my son. It will help you forget this day ever happened."

Angrily, Chou knocked the pipe to the floor. With no further words, the sobbing patriarch stormed off to his study to seek solace in a bottle of expensive gwai lah whisky, rather than his mother's opium.

Chapter 5

During the ensuing weeks, Chou brooded about the farm while continuing on with the farm's daily operations. He seldom spoke to his family, often sitting in his study during the evening meal, causing his already small-framed body to take on a gaunt appearance.

Neither Chou nor anyone else in the Gong family would speak Jun's name. But their wayward son weighed heavily in the thoughts of all the family members as they listened nightly to the news on the radio of the relentless advance of the Japanese army.

"Will the Japanese hurt us?" Mi inquired at dinner one evening.

"The Japanese are of the same blood as us, Mi," said Zu in a reassuring voice. "They look just like us, daughter. They will not harm us."

"Then Mother, why are they in China? The radio said..."

"Pay no attention to the damn radio news. News people always make things sound more serious than they really are," Chou interrupted.

Ree didn't agree. "The Japanese must be in China for a reason, Father. I think we're all in danger. If all of the Generalissimo's soldiers are like I-goo, we will be lucky if any Chinese in Kiangsu Province survive."

Suddenly, Ree felt the sting of her father's hand across her cheek.

"You foolish girl. Do not worry your younger sister in that manner. True, the Japanese want things that China possesses, but they will not harm us as long as we give them what they want. They will not take everything we possess, only what they need, and then they will leave." Chou's voice was harsh and scolding.

Showing little emotion, Ree wiped a small trickle of blood from the corner of her mouth with the back of her hand. She silently rose up from the dinner table and retired to her bedroom. The remaining members of the Gong family continued to eat their meal in silence. It was not the first time the patriarch had struck Ree. She resented that her father had never once struck his precious son. In the past she would have defiantly cursed Chou, but she was now numb to the abuse.

Chou's heated outburst was a result of the stress over the loss of Jun and the formidable enemy that would soon be upon them. He felt deeply ashamed about striking his eldest daughter and chastising her, but being the head of the family, he found it difficult to apologize, especially to any female.

A few days later the first chill of late autumn gave notice that the winter melons were ready for harvest. Any resentment, guilt, or hostility amongst the Gong family was put aside to concentrate on the arduous task of harvesting.

As a custom, the first melon picked would have the honor of being the first course of a grand meal to commemorate the beginning of the harvest. Sir Justin Farnsworth, the British ambassador to China, and his seventeen-year-old daughter, Sylvia, were customarily invited to join the Gongs for the auspicious dinner.

With trepidation, Ree would be required by her parents to wear an expensive lo fon evening gown her mother had purchased from an English clothing catalog. And with equal loathing she was made to wear ill-fitting dress shoes upon her normally bare feet.

"My God, sister dear," mocked Mi as the two dressed for the elegant dinner. "You actually have tits! Since you mostly wear those loose-fitting boys' shirts most of the time, I was unsure whether I had one or two brothers."

"Who are you to criticize, little sister?" Ree retorted. "You have the figure of a chopstick. In addition, you and Jun have never had to rise before dawn or feel the sweat of honest labor in your lives."

"Bitch!" Mi said sharply. "I am a female of upper-class, and I plan to marry a man even richer than our father. You are just jealous because I am the pretty one in the family. Our father is rich. I do not have to work. Why do you waste your time in the fields when you could be flirting with the cute boys of rich Nanking families?"

"Shut up, little sister. My life is my life."

A loud knock abruptly ended their heated conversation. It was Mother Zu. "What are you two arguing over now? Stop the squabbling and come down at once. Our guests have just arrived. It would be rude not to greet them immediately."

"Yes, Mother," Mi said, not wanting her mother to know of the disharmony between her and Ree. She opened the door for Ree. "After you, bitch."

"Thank you, whore," responded Ree.

As the two girls descended the stairway, the British ambassador gleefully exclaimed, "I am indeed gazing at the two most beautiful girls in Kiangsu Province!"

"Father, I heartily agree," daughter Sylvia concurred. "My best friend Ree and her sister Mi are undoubtedly the most beautiful girls in all China."

"But of course, my lovely daughter is the most beautiful *foreign* girl residing in China," added the ambassador, to spare any slighted feelings.

"All right, we're all beautiful, Sir Farnsworth," joked Ree. "So let's forget the compliments and eat. I'm starving."

"Ree! Your abruptness to Sir Farnsworth is unconscionable," scolded Chou, embarrassed. "My apologies, Sir Farnsworth. It is perhaps ill-breeding, or perhaps a few drops of Mongol blood are in her."

Chuckling with great amusement, the balding and rotund British gentleman caressed Ree's cheek. "Your daughter is quite unique, as well as lovely. You need not apologize. For far too long we Limeys have adhered to silly, rigid protocol. Your daughter only wished to open our eyes to such foolishness. By the way, as I have stated before, my first name is Justin, not Sir Farnsworth. So let's dine, shall we, as your daughter distinctly stated?"

"Justin, then you must call me Chou. Do not forget the Chinese custom of first name last, last name first," Chou interjected.

Justin took his daughter's arm on one side and Ree's on the other. Together the trio strolled into the dining room, followed by the rest of the Gong family.

Flickering candles attached to sterling silver holders bathed the diners' faces with a soft yellow glow. Going against custom, Chou insisted the ambassador sit at the head of the table—a seat usually reserved for the family patriarch. This Chou did out of respect and some feeling of inferiority toward Farnsworth's high position, and the mere fact that he was a gwai lah.

Though the ambassador felt somewhat awkward sitting at the head of the table, he did not wish to say or do anything that might offend his dear friend, so he accepted his seat graciously.

Once everyone was seated, an elderly servant woman slowly pushed a squeaky dining cart from the kitchen. On it was an immense, hollowed-out and intricately carved winter melon. Steaming broth, cubes of melon flesh, Chinese red dates, bits of pork, and black mushrooms filled the cavity.

"What a pleasant aroma, Chou," Justin said as the servant woman filled their bowls. "This winter melon soup is truly worthy of the King of England."

"Thank you, Sir Farns—uh, Justin," chortled Chou. "We are so honored you and your beautiful daughter have come to our harvest dinner again this year."

"What news do you have of the Japanese invasion?" inquired Zu.

"Your great General Chiang and his capable army are pushing those horrid Japanese back to their island kingdom. Your fearless leader has assured me of an eventual Chinese victory over them." He chuckled, trying to lighten the conversation. "Your family and the people of Nanking are in no danger. The fact that the Japanese have horns growing out the tops of their heads is no reason to fear them. Incidentally," he added, "I ran across your son Jun the other day. He is becoming a first-rate soldier."

"Do not speak of Jun. He is a stranger to me," Chou said coldly. "I do not know a man named Jun. This man is an opium addict and a failure."

With a newfound courage, Mama On sprang up from the dinner table. "Do not speak of your son—my grandson—as if he no longer exists. It is not his fault he has a fondness for opium. I was the one who introduced him to it. You wanted him to live up to such high expectations, but it was not in him. Why could you not leave him alone to be part of the furniture, like us Gong women?"

Chou's eyes drilled menacingly at his mother. "Mother, sit down and finish your meal. You are behaving like a foolish old woman in front of our honored guests. Jun is a man. Women bear children and tend to the running of the household, but a man has more pressing obligations. Justin, my friend, God is a man, yes?"

Justin stared at his bowl of simmering winter melon soup uncomfortably. "Well, yes Chou, but..."

A loud knock on the door cut short the ambassador's reply.

A servant opened the door to find a very agitated Lieutenant Song, his uniform tattered and dust-laden.

"I must speak to Mr. Gong! Immediately!" screamed

Song.

Before the servant could reply, the young officer barged his way into the dining room, the old woman following close behind, cursing his rude boldness.

"Lieutenant Song, have you come to slap us around again?" Chou said flippantly.

Before responding, Song took hold of one of the wine glasses resting on the table. The flustered young man began gulping down the wine, spilling much of it on his tunic.

"Help yourself to my wine," mused Chou.

"Damn it, young man!" screeched Mama On impatiently. "Please come to the point. Our dinner is growing cold."

Lieutenant Song paused to catch his breath, then said gravely, "Very well. Our enemy is now very near. So near that you will soon feel the monster's breath against your neck."

A look of complete shock came across the faces of all the Gong family members, as well as the ambassador and his daughter.

"How close is close?" asked Chou.

"The Japanese forces will be at the gates of Nanking in forty-eight hours, perhaps less," Song estimated grimly.

"Surely the Generalissimo's army will stop them," said the ambassador.

Song rolled his eyes at the ambassador's ludicrous remark. "Our fearless leader, at this very moment, is making preparations to retreat up river 1,200 miles to Chongqing. He plans to make Chongqing the new provisional capitol of China. Our God-like leader is just as afraid of the enemy as everyone else in China. The emperor is naked—is that not how you lo fons would term it? I ask all of you once again to please leave Kiangsu Province. Do not dawdle," the young man pleaded.

"The sky is falling, the sky is falling!" Chou quoted from a lo fon nursery story.

"Mr. Gong, you are failing to understand the seriousness of the situation," Song stated.

"The lieutenant is right, my friend. If this is so, you and your family must leave the province at once," said Ambassador Farnsworth. "Your lives are most certainly in danger."

A puzzled look crossed Chou's face. "Justin, it was you who just reassured us that the Generalissimo and his army had the Japanese well in hand."

Justin looked glum. "My friends, I was speaking in little white lies so you would not worry. But now—now we must face reality."

"Father, our melons," Ree said anxiously. "What is to become of our winter melons?"

The ambassador's daughter eyed Ree with foreboding fear. "Ree, dear girlfriend," Sylvia said, "the melons are the least of your worries. Your family farm lies directly in the path of the onrushing Japanese army. I love you, Ree. If you will not leave Kiangsu, at least come with me and Father to the British Embassy compound. You will be safe there, this I promise you." She clutched Ree's hands strongly. "Furthermore, you and Mi have not attended school in ages. My private tutor can help you both with basic learning."

"May I say, honored friend," Ambassador Farnsworth said to Chou, "my daughter's invitation also applies to you and all of your family. There are reports of the brutalities of the Japanese soldiers. Atrocities that I cannot speak of in polite company. I have diplomatic immunity. The British Embassy is considered British soil. As my daughter so stated, you will be safe there."

Chou felt mixed emotions over the ambassador's generous offer. Being the proud patriarch of a prominent family, it was awkward for him to accept charity from anyone, especially a gwai lah. But at the same time he knew that his family's position was very precarious.

Chou pondered his decision for a moment. He would not allow his pride to be tarnished by accepting a handout from anyone, despite the danger it might place him and his family in if he refused. "You're too kind, my lo fon friend, but I think the reports of the Japanese offenses are exaggerated. The Japanese and the Chinese are of the same blood. They will not exploit us or humiliate us as you gwai lahs have done to us for centuries," Chou said adamantly. "And you insult me by offering my daughters an education. They are women. They do not need an education. My family and I will stay to complete the harvest, and that is my absolute last word on this issue."

"Fool!" scolded Mama On. "You are allowing your ridiculous male pride get in the way of your family's safety. At least allow the girls to stay at the embassy."

Chou looked at his mother with a scowl. "Your tongue has become quite sharp in your old age, my dear mother. Like my father, I alone will make the decisions which I feel are best for the family. But," he finished, "I will ask one favor of my gwai lah friend."

"Of course," replied the ambassador. "Anything, my good friend."

"I have bond certificates in several lo fon Blue Chip companies. It amounts to a rather large sum of money. Can I entrust you to keep these certificates safe for me until this crisis is over?"

"Most assuredly. You can trust me, old friend. You have my word on it as an English gentleman. I apologize for my daughter. It was not her place to offer your daughters an education."

"Apology accepted," Chou said with a chuckle. "I do believe you're an honorable man, even if you are gwai lah. If it should be my fate that I cannot survive this ordeal, please do your best to see that Jun takes possession of the certificates, my friend."

The ambassador displayed a rather perplexed look upon hearing Chou's request. "I beg your pardon, dear chap. I was under the impression that you are estranged with your son. If, God forbid, you should meet your demise in the near future, do you not suppose your daughters will have need of the certificates, as well?"

The patriarch Chou glared with great insult at the ambassador's candid question. "True, my son is weak and he has contributed little to the running of the family farm. And thanks to his grandmother, my son is also an opium addict. But a son is a son. Daughters have no value to me whatsoever. Jun is my son. He bears the last name of Gong. When my daughters marry, they will take another name, and the Gong name will die with my son should he perish before siring children!" Chou shrieked in defiance.

"Mr. Gong, your daughters are your own flesh and blood!" Sylvia cut in sharply. "They deserve your assets as much as, if not more than, your uncaring, ill-mannered son. Gong is only a name. What name a person goes by has no bearing on how much family members love one another."

"Sylvia, you need not defend my sister and me," Ree lamented. "It has been explained to the both of us countless times throughout our lives that people without a growth between their legs are of little value. You need not speak for Mi and myself. We are not worthy of it."

"Preposterous!" exclaimed Sylvia. "You are both the children of Chou and Zu. The same blood flows through both son and daughters. A dangling appendage between one's legs does not make one far superior."

"Sylvia!" the ambassador scolded. "You forget that you are an English lady and a guest in Mr. Gong's house. Your behavior is inexcusable. Behave yourself, or we shall leave at once!"

Chou smiled with minor amusement. "Justin, kind friend, thank you for coming to my defense. Your daughter has been associated with Ree for too long. I must accept some blame for her behavior. I did not beat Ree enough when she was a child." Half joking and half serious, he finished, "What a pity female foot binding is now illegal in China."

Outraged by her father's lack of regard for his two daughters, Ree had reached her breaking point. "Father, it is a bit too late for that," Ree said. "With luck the Japanese will kill me. Then I will no longer be a burden to you. Officer Song, will you be good enough to drive me to Nanking?"

"Certainly," replied the young officer.

"What will you do in Nanking?" Zu asked with a very worried look.

"Mother, I haven't the slightest idea," Ree replied caustically. "Perhaps a whore. That is what Father seems to think all women are, anyway."

"Let her go," Chou said with equal hostility. "She will not be gone long. Once my oldest daughter sees just how difficult life is outside these walls she will beg me to accept her back."

Quickly Ree hugged her mother, grandmother, and sister.

"Granddaughter," Mama On said, "take my wool sweater. You will need it." She placed it over Ree's shoulders.

"Please stay, Ree," begged a tearful Zu.

"Ree, my beloved friend, go to the British embassy," said Sylvia. "I will protect you."

Ree looked lovingly into Sylvia's eyes, wrapped her arms around the equally tall blond, and kissed her best friend on the lips. But she did not respond to her mother's pleas or to Sylvia's request. She simply turned and walked out the front door with Officer Song.

Chou sipped his tea unemotionally and gazed blandly at an autographed portrait of Tz'u-Hsi, the last empress of China. Finally, he broke the silence: "My honored guests, I apologize for the interruption. Now, let us continue with our fine meal."

Chapter 6

Clothed in her expensive evening gown, Ree boarded Song's military car. The vehicle raced westward toward Nanking. Ree's mind was racing right along with it. *I am only seventeen,* she thought. *What an idiot I must be to leave my family! My father has slighted and insulted me my whole life. What is one more insult upon a great dung-heap of insults?*

When they reached the city outskirts, Ree and Song were greeted by a long stream of Nanking citizenry fleeing the city, and a near equal portion of humanity moving into the city.

"How strange and funny it seems that as many people wish to enter Nanking as wish to leave," Ree remarked.

"Most who enter the city are frightened peasants with nowhere else to go," Song commented. "And while a great portion of the city people are leaving, a large portion are staying, as well. They believe Nanking's sixty-foot-high walls will save them from the Japanese. But those thick walls did not protect our ancestors from the Mongols many centuries ago, and they are not likely to offer any better protection against a modern army."

"And yet you stay?" Ree asked.

"I am a soldier. It is my duty to die needlessly for a leader who cannot save China. The only difference between the Generalissimo and the Japanese is that he is not destroying China at gunpoint," Song reflected.

"Before you die needlessly, shall we finish our tea party?" Ree said with a touch of cynicism.

Song chuckled. "The world is coming to an end and you wish to drink tea?"

"Why not?" asked Ree. "Is there nothing more we could do before the world ends?"

"There is nothing else that comes to mind," Song laughed.

They threaded their way through the swelling crowds until they reached the city wall. They stopped at the same spot where they had had their first tea atop the wall. The frenzied scene was a sharp contrast to the tranquil environment of only a few weeks earlier.

Reaching the top of the wall, the couple was welcomed by a number of soldiers busily preparing a defense against the enemy juggernaut. The men, noticing a soldier of superior rank, stood sharply at attention and saluted Lieutenant Song.

Song returned the salute. "Gentleman, for the moment you will stop what you are doing. You are hereby ordered to go to the street and direct traffic. The streets are a madhouse and need order. I will call on you shortly."

"But sir, we have orders to—"

"Do not challenge my authority!" Song screamed.

"Yes, sir!" trembled the corporal as he and the others tripped over each other, descending the hand-hewn stone steps with haste.

Ree and Song grinned, fighting back their laughter.

"You play God very well," mused Ree.

Song pulled a silver liquor flask from his back pocket. "With such short notice, we'll have to improvise, and use sherry instead of tea," he said as he unscrewed the cap.

"Song, why have you not called on me in so many weeks?" Ree inquired.

Song took a long gulp from his sherry-filled flask. "I may act like God to my men," he said, "but I am a frightened child to tall thin women with sharp tongues." He handed the flask to Ree.

"I would not think God has a pockmarked face or that he would fear a lowly woman," Ree giggled, drawing a short measure of sherry.

Song took hold of Ree's left hand. His face was troubled. "The enemy is at the gate and you have nowhere to go. At least you could have gone to the British embassy. But your damn pride—like that of a man—will not allow you to do so. What could you possibly have been thinking, to leave your family so abruptly without a net to catch you if you fall?"

Ree laughed softly under her breath. "And like a man, I act without thinking of the consequences. If you were to call me an idiot, you would not get an argument from me." She lifted the flask in a toast. "Here is to both our salvations, my honorable soldier," said Ree, taking a long swallow. She began choking on the strong liquor.

Song slapped her back to aid her breathing. "You act as though you have never had spirits before," he laughed.

Ree grinned with embarrassment. "I have only had strong drinks once before, a few months ago at my grandmother's seventieth birthday dinner," she said between coughs.

"Then drink more cautiously," Song warned, amused. "The potent sherry will grow you some balls, and when the enemy arrives you will need them. And you will forget that I have a pockmarked face and we will both begin to look much better to each other."

Giggling, Ree said, "I was only mocking you for amusement. You are a beautiful man. In low light one cannot even see the little craters on your cheeks."

Song smiled. "And you are even more beautiful with a washed face and wearing a dress."

Despite the great chaos surrounding them, Ree and Song had become too enthralled with each other to notice anything but themselves. Additionally, the sherry had dulled their reasoning. The two of them giggled as if they were children again, gazing sharply into one another's eyes. Ree took the near-empty flask and turned it upside down. She placed her fingers under the spout. A single drop of sherry sluggishly fell onto her fingers. Ree created a thin film of the liquid on her thumb and index finger, then gently pressed her moist fingers across Song's lips. Her heart began to beat so rapidly she thought that Song must surely hear it.

In a sudden, impulsive burst, Ree joined her lips to Songs. True to Song's words, the strong liquor had stripped away her inhibitions.

Ree and Song knelt down as if they were one being. Ree leaned back upon the cold and weathered walkway with Song's body straddling her. For the first time in her life, Ree felt a true sense of freedom. The touch of a young man's lithe and sinewy body against her own youthful body was like nothing she had experienced before. Her nipples hardened as she felt the hardness between Song's legs. Neither wanted to release the other, and they both prayed the moment wouldn't end.

While the couple's rapture became more and more intense, the muffled reports of artillery and small weapon fire were becoming more and more pronounced with each passing second.

"Lieutenant Song, you never told me your first name," Ree said.

"Tai," he whispered in her ear.

"Uh...a thousand apologies, sir...uh..."

A flustered subordinate soldier stood over the pair. "You and the lady must stop what you are doing. It is not safe here. I would be most honored to escort your lady friend to the Nanking City Hall. She would be out of immediate danger there," pleaded the soldier.

Disturbed by the interruption, Song gazed angrily up at the meddling soldier. "Sergeant, can you not see that the lady and I are busy? You need not concern yourself with our welfare," he said in a sherry-tainted voice.

The embarrassed soldier saluted. "My regrets, sir.

I..."

His sentence abruptly halted as shrapnel from an exploding artillery shell tore through his head. In surreal horror, Ree and Song watched the top of his head blow apart, raining myriad small bits of flesh, blood, and brain matter across their faces and clothes. His near-headless body fell atop the reclining couple.

"Dear God!" Song exclaimed, pushing the soldier off of them. "We are in danger." He turned to Ree. "The poor man was also right that you must go to the city hall. With luck, the Generalissimo will offer you protection."

A stunned Ree removed a bit of the sergeant's brain from her cheek. Once realizing what it was, she began to scream hysterically.

Song lifted Ree off the ground and shook his panicked lover. "Country girl! Get a hold of yourself! You're a strong woman and you will survive if you keep your wits about you," he lectured over the exploding artillery shells overhead.

"Yes, Tai," Ree said, regaining her composure. "We must keep our wits to survive. And you must promise me you will also survive."

"Ree, I will stay alive for you and you only, that I promise. Now, take hold of my hand and do not let go," Song said with a reassuring voice. He led Ree down to the street.

With the enemy almost at the gates of Nanking, the chaotic street scene had escalated to total pandemonium.

Chapter 7

The streets of Nanking were strewn with injured and dead civilians and Nationalist soldiers, many of which had not succumbed to the enemy shells, but had been trampled by the feet of thousands of people fleeing the city, or rushing to the center of Nanking with the foolish belief that China's leader would protect them. Ree and Song began to descend the stairs, clutching each other's hands.

"Wait! Wait—" Ree said, trying to pull Song back up the steps. "We must go back and bring the sergeant down. He needs medical attention," she said irrationally.

"God has already helped the sergeant by taking him away from this place of horror," Song responded. He dragged his stubborn lover to the street level.

"It's hopeless," Ree observed. "What are we to do, Song?"

"Hold on, my love," replied an anguished Song. "Do not let go, no matter what. It is too congested for us to drive. We will have to walk to City Hall."

Cautiously, the couple edged into the flow of crazed citizens. At a snail's pace they moved in the direction of City Hall, all the while the endless explosions of artillery shells violating their ears. People leapt to their deaths from high buildings rather than face the uncertainties of enemy occupation. Ree held onto Song tightly, knowing her life depended on it.

"Make way! Make way!" Song shouted, firing his pistol into the air. "I am an officer of the Nationalist Army! Make way!"

Taking two hours to span only a few blocks, City Hall was now in sight. A wall of armed Nationalist soldiers precariously held back the swarm of people begging for entry, crying out the Generalissimo's name and pleading for protection from the invading Japanese.

"Tang!" cried Song, waving his military cap in an attempt to gain the attention of a comrade who was commanding the sentries. Song, a tall man wearing a Nationalist uniform, was spotted by his friend and colleague. The commander ordered his men to make a path for the lieutenant and his female companion. A contingent of troops waded into the packed crowd, striking with batons anyone who did not move quickly enough to suit them.

"Bastards!" shrieked Ree, appalled by the soldiers' actions. "It is not necessary for your fellow soldiers to injure women and old men."

"Song, China's favorite son, what brings you and your lovely lady friend to City Hall?" asked Tang once the couple reached the makeshift barrier.

"Tang, my friend, this young woman is a Gong. Her father is one of the most important people in Kiangsu Province. Please, I beg you. Will you help her? She and her family need protection from the invaders."

Tang rolled his eyes in exasperation. "Who the hell doesn't need protection from the Japs? Let me guess: You wish me to take your lady friend to the Generalissimo." He laughed. "The Generalissimo is indisposed. I would have difficulty getting God in to see him on such a day."

Song placed his hands on Tang's shoulders. "Tang, my loyal friend, at least try to get her an audience with the Generalissimo. You know very well what the Japanese do to women."

"All right, I will try," Tang replied.

Feeling relieved, Song turned toward the woman he was beginning to value more than his own life. With sorrowful eyes, he looked into Ree's eyes. "I must now leave to battle our enemies. Do not die—I order you. As you've said, we must finish our tea."

Ree pulled Song against her, wanting to remember the contours and ripples of every inch of his taut body. "It's a mad world, Song. I also command you to stay alive," she whispered.

"This war should not last long. Meet me on the wall where we had our first 'date,' as the gwai lahs term it, when this insanity ends," said Song.

"Indeed, I will be there," Ree reassured him.

With a brief kiss, Song turned away and melted into the swarming masses.

"Miss, come with me," Tang said, tugging at Ree's arm.

Gripped with cold fear, Ree could not help but wonder if she would ever see Song or her family again. In addition, the violent death of the young soldier replayed over and over in her mind. Walking morosely, Ree was escorted by Song's friend and another soldier to the Generalissimo's apartment suite. The overbearing barking of China's leader giving countless orders could be heard from far down the hallway.

"Miss, wait here while I announce your presence to the Generalissimo," said Tang.

Lacking patience and not being one to stand on etiquette, Ree barged into the Generalissimo's suite rather than wait to be announced. In her haste, she knocked over a servant carrying a stack of government papers, scattering them across the floor.

The Generalissimo's guards wrestled the impudent young woman to the ground.

"Generalissimo!" Ree said desperately. "Remember me? Gong Ree? I must speak with you at once. It is urgent."

"Yes, of course I remember you," the Generalissimo said. "You're the young woman with testicles like a man." He waved at his guards. "Gentlemen, release her. Assist her off of the floor." He began to sort through a stack of papers, not even bothering to look at Ree. "Young lady, with you it is always urgent. Please be brief. I am pressed for time."

"Please, I ask you—I *beg* you, honorable leader of my country—please send some of your troops to protect my family. The Japanese will surely pass through my family's farm en route to Nanking."

A thin smile crossed the Generalissimo's thin face. "Protect and serve!" he said. Finally he looked directly at Ree. "Dear lady, I have 300 million Chinese citizens to save. I cannot save you all. Millions will die, but China itself will not. That is the sad truth of war," said the Generalissimo. He circled Ree curiously, running his fingers through her jet back hair. "Miss Gong, I cannot save you all, however you are a pretty young woman of child-bearing age. China will need such fertile young ladies to replenish its population. You will accompany me to Chongqing. I will protect you. In fact," he said, whispering lecherously into Ree's ear, "you will be under my personal care. To serve me is to serve China."

"Sir, you shame me and you shame China," Ree said. "You are raping China just as the Japanese are." She shook her head. "Who should I fear more, you or the invaders?"

The leader glared at the young woman with an arrogant smugness. "Young lady," the Generalissimo replied, "you do not understand the difficulty in leading such an enormous and diverse country like China. I have only love for my country. Only I can drive the Japanese out of China. Then I will destroy the Communists, the other cancer of China. But these goals cannot be accomplished today. I must now retreat with the bulk of my army still intact to Chongqing. I will transfer the nation's capitol there, regroup, and direct the war from that city. You are far too young and naïve to understand what is happening to this country," he added. "Someday you will understand. Pray for China."

"And this expensive furniture your men are packing for transport, you need these things to defeat the Japanese?" Ree retorted, snatching a Ming vase off of a pedestal and smashing it to the floor.

"Damn it, girl! Do you know how much that vase was worth?" cried the Generalissimo.

"To you more than the lives of China," Ree said. "I saw a man's head explode today. Fearless leader, you speak of saving China, but you could not prevent a skinny teenage girl from breaking one of your precious vases."

"Insolent, lowly female!" shrieked the Generalissimo. "If I were not pressed for time I would have you shot for such insolence. You will see many more heads explode before I can drive the Japanese from China." Chiang fought the urge to strike the girl, and an exasperated frown crossed the face of the man accustomed to being surrounded by sycophants. An exasperated frown crossed the leader's face. "Young lady, can you not understand China stands alone? The gangster gwai lah Roosevelt will not help us. In fact, the entire world cares little about the fate of our country. *Si-lent le-ges in-ter ar-na*," he enunciated. "I was speaking in Latin; 'The laws are silent in the midst of arms.' Good day, Miss Gong. Stay out of harm's way."

He turned his back to Ree and resumed his preparations for his departure to Chongqing.

Ree stood staring with disbelief at the man who millions of people worshipped as a god. She now realized for certain that Chiang Kai-shek was a delusional paper tiger living in his own world.

"God help me...God help China," Ree muttered under her breath as she hastily left the Generalissimo's suite. "If God exists—the one Sylvia told me of."

Stunned by the brutal death of the sergeant and her

failure to coax China's leader into protecting her family, Ree wandered aimlessly around the city.

I never should have left my family, she thought. *We should die together. I must go back.* Thoughts flooded her mind. *Will I ever see Song again? He is the only man I have ever felt close to. He can be strong-headed and temperamental...*she giggled out loud. *He reminds me of me.*

Thousands joined Ree, roaming the streets with blank stares and vacant eyes, not knowing what the future would bring. Some looted abandoned stores and residences while most stood idly by, too frightened or complacent to care. Many cried or spoke to themselves.

Ree felt deeply for all the panicked people that surrounded her, but she knew there was nothing she could do to help them. She was probably destined to meet the same horrid fate as all of them. Ree felt a tugging at her skirt. She looked down to find an elderly woman, weeping.

"Miss, kill me. Kill me, please," said the old woman in a weak and frightened voice. "I do not want to be raped or slaughtered by the devils from Japan. Please...please. I beg you."

Ree stood speechless, overwhelmed by the magnitude of the tragic events unfolding around her. *How can people be so desperate as to want their lives to end rather than face an unknown enemy?* she thought.

She took a firm grip on the old woman's hands and sat down beside her on the curb. She then removed the heavy wool sweater her grandmother had given her and placed it over the old woman's shoulders.

"Dear lady, I wish I could grant you your request, but I do not have the stomach to take a person's life, though it might be merciful if I did. Our powerful Generalissimo will save us all," Ree said, hoping to give the old woman a bit of hope, even though she knew it was false.

Ree wiped the tears from the old woman's cheeks.

The woman gave her a brave smile in return. Fighting back her own tears, Ree rose from the street curb and walked away, knowing there was little else she could do for the woman.

"Like our soulless leader, I can do nothing to help anyone," Ree whispered under her breath. She knew she had few options. Her only choice was to somehow return to the family farm. With luck she would find her family unharmed, though she knew that was a remote possibility. In any case, she had to know how her family had fared after the intruders passed through the Gong farm.

Ree also thought of Song. She envisioned his body against hers. A brief smile appeared on her face as she walked through the chaotic madness. Though the young couple had groped and fondled each other atop the Nanking wall, their relationship had not been consummated. Ree was still a virgin. She laughed, pondering how large Song's manhood might be.

As she made her way toward the east wall, Ree noticed something was strangely amiss. It dawned on her that the loud, repeated firing of artillery shells and small arms fire had stopped. *Did Chiang's army actually driven the invaders away?* she wondered optimistically. But she knew her hopes were only an unrealistic fantasy.

Turning a corner, she was confronted by row upon row of the Generalissimo's soldiers, standing submissively before the victorious Japanese enemy. A pompous-looking Japanese officer paraded up and down each row of soldiers, violently striking the face of any Chinese soldier who dared weep or speak out. Thousands of civilians stood by, witnessing the humiliating scene.

"Bastards!" Ree exclaimed. "They gave up without a proper fight. Perhaps they cannot be blamed for the defeat. They had a foolish and vain leader to guide them."

Like all of the other bystanders, Ree stood

mesmerized by the first close-up sighting of their conquerors.

"Ninety-thousand Nationalist troops our competent Generalissimo left behind," said one elderly Chinese man, weeping, "and they could not defend Nanking from this small force. How disgraceful."

A single shot rang out from atop the city wall, commanding the attention of the thousands of civilians and Chinese soldiers standing on the street below. Ree looked upward and saw a stout Japanese officer with tea-colored skin and narrow, unemotional eyes, gazing down at his captives. Speaking in a forceful, god-like fashion, the Japanese commander introduced himself and explained the present situation.

"To the people of Nanking, and the soldiers of Nationalist China: My name is Colonel Isao Ito of the Imperial Japanese Army. You are all prisoners of the Empire of Japan. I wish to make it quite clear to every man, woman, and child of Nanking that you will display at all times an absolute obedience and courtesy to myself and the army of the occupying Japanese forces. To show any act of discourtesy or disobedience whatsoever to any of my men will result in an immediate execution. To make my point very clear, and so that there is no confusion on your part as to my orders, I have asked my men to pick out ten of your cowardly protectors at random."

Three Japanese soldiers quickly yanked ten Chinese soldiers from the long lines. Ree, along with thousands of onlookers, gasped in horror as the men's hands were tied behind their backs and they were ordered down onto their knees.

A young woman ran out of the massive crowd. She approached a sergeant, identifying herself as the wife of one of the condemned soldiers. In near hysteria the woman took hold of the sergeant's tunic, begging for her husband's life.

The sergeant brushed her aside. "Your husband, like all of China's soldiers, is a eunuch. And China's women are whores. You must give your Japanese guests a proper greeting."

Grinning widely, the sergeant grasped the woman's arms and pushed her down onto her knees. He took hold of her head as though it were a cantaloupe and pressed her face into his crotch. The other Japanese soldiers roared with laughter at the young woman's humiliation.

Her husband stood up in protest. A rifle shot echoed off the city wall and the tall surrounding buildings. The woman's husband died instantly as the bullet tore an obscene wound through his face.

The Generalissimo was right, Ree thought. *I will see other heads explode.* She gawked at the horrific actions of the invaders with bewilderment. *Why would men of any nation be so cruel to the people of another nation? What do they hope to gain from all this?* thought Ree.

The crowd stood in stunned shock as the sergeant ordered the execution of the other nine kneeling soldiers. A Japanese soldier with a pistol in his hand stepped slowly down the line, shooting each kneeling man in the back of the head. When he had spent his six rounds, he drew his samurai sword and decapitated the four remaining Chinese men with swift swipes of his blade. The Chinese citizens watched helplessly as, one by one, the men toppled like dominoes. Many of the onlookers fainted at the sight of the severed heads and splattered blood on the cobblestone square.

Chapter 8

Many wept while others pleaded for mercy as the Japanese sergeant continued his lecture. "It is a great dishonor for a soldier to surrender to an enemy. A true soldier and a true man does not stop fighting until he has breathed his final breath, and his heart has made its final beat."

While the others stood in timid silence, Ree stepped forward to speak out, oblivious about the risk. "Murderers! Monsters! Who do you think you are?"

The Japanese sergeant looked around with surprise. He seemed amused that his condemner was a lanky, teenage girl. He chuckled. "Little girl, I am Sergeant 'the horse' Suzuki Toro of the Imperial Japanese Army, that is who I am. I am your god. You will live and die at my whim," he said in a raspy voice.

"How odd. I didn't think God would be so foul-smelling and I envisioned him to be at least a foot taller. Why are you named 'Horse'? Because your face resembles one?"

The sergeant grabbed Ree and pushed her to the ground. He stood in a towering shadow over her. "I am nicknamed 'Horse' because I have the sexual organ of one. I did not receive a proper greeting from your fellow countrywoman, but I suspect you will be a better hostess," Suzuki retorted, dropping his pants.

Frozen with fear, Ree closed her eyes tightly as the squatty, muscular man climbed on top of her. Desperately she clawed at the sergeant's pock-marked face. Suzuki groped under Ree's dress and took hold of her under garment, pulling it down to her knees. In a final act to break free, Ree maneuvered her face closer to the side of Suzuki's head. Feeling the contour of his beard-stubbled face, Ree bit down on his left ear, severing its fleshy lobe.

Blood covered Ree's chin and neck as she spit out the piece of Suzuki's ear. Crying out in pain, the sergeant began beating Ree's face without mercy.

Nearly unconscious, Ree faintly heard the cries of an elderly woman. With blood blurring her vision, Ree saw a familiar face. It was the old woman she had given her wool sweater to.

"Leave her alone, you filthy man!" shouted the woman, pounding her frail fists against the sergeant's back.

"Mettlesome old witch," Suzuki said. "Damn you!" He took hold of his samurai sword and stood up. He pushed his face to within a few inches of the old woman's. Standing her ground, she fearlessly spat into the sergeant's face. With a swift swipe of his finely sharpened blade, Suzuki severed the old woman's head.

Ree watched the head bounce along the cobblestone street like a cabbage fallen from a vegetable cart. "No!" she screamed. "No!"

Many of the Chinese bystanders became violently ill after witnessing the monstrous act. Acting as though he had just swatted a fly, Suzuki casually took a clean cloth from his pocket and began to wipe the dripping blood from his cherished sword.

Ree knew that Suzuki would again turn his attention toward her. She lifted a loose stone from the street and struck Suzuki across the side of the head. The heavily-built man fell forward. Ree jumped to her feet and fled in fear, melting into the immense crowd of Chinese civilians. Coming to Ree's aid, her fellow countrymen and women wedged themselves together, forming a human wall between Ree and the Japanese soldiers.

Ree raced down shadowy alleyways until her legs felt so stiff and heavy that she could not take another step. She found a vacant building and broke into it, praying that she could seek shelter from a world gone mad.

In a dark, bare room, Ree cowered into a corner. Her once fine evening gown was now tattered and blood-stained. She pulled her knees up and covered her face, closing her eyes tightly.

I am only seventeen, what did I do to deserve this? Ree thought.

She wondered about home, her family, the rich soil that she toiled in so much of her life, and her winter melons. She reflected on the spring planting with her father, though they were never close. For the first time in her life, Ree felt truly alone.

The sun was quickly setting, robbing what little light that filtered into her secret hiding place. Sitting in silence, the seconds seemed like minutes and the minutes seemed like hours. The endless, morose noises of the dying, the buzzing of enemy planes, and the shouting of Japanese soldiers pierced into her soul like needles. Any moment Ree expected Sergeant Suzuki to enter her feeble sanctuary and, with his long sword, sever her head in the same fashion as he'd done with the old woman. Frozen in her little corner, Ree huddled for hours, unable to move.

As midnight approached, a light pierced the vacant room. Ree could make out the voices speaking in foreign tongues. It was the Japanese troops, searching for civilians and deserters who didn't want to surrender to them. The lead soldier directed his flashlight beam over every square inch of the room. Ree shook violently with fear, knowing that the light would eventually find her in one of the corners. Not wanting to face her inevitable discovery, Ree leapt to her feet and charged directly into the blinding light. Catching the startled soldiers off guard, Ree bowled over the lead soldier, knocking him backward against his two comrades, causing all three to topple.

With the speed of youth on her side, Ree reached the street before the soldiers could stand up. Ignoring their shouts for her to stop, Ree ran until it felt as though her lungs would burst. She stopped for a moment to catch her breath. Looking around, she spied a hole in the city wall, just a short distance away, created by an artillery shell. Climbing over fist-sized rubble, Ree clawed her way through the opening and out of the city proper.

Her only thoughts now were of the welfare of her family and of the winter melon farm she loved so dearly. Walking parallel to the road, Ree began the thirty-mile journey back to the family farm under the cloak of darkness, all the while observing the constant stream of military traffic heading toward Nanking. As daylight neared, Ree found shelter in a culvert near a shallow stream. Her body shook as she fought off the morning chill.

Despite all that had transpired, Ree could not help but smile, thinking how she wished she still had the heavy wool sweater she had given the old woman. "That old woman gave her life for me," Ree whispered to herself.

After a fitful rest, Ree awakened to the annoying drone of military planes flying overhead.

They sound like buzzing bees, she thought as she watched the planes.

The bombers appeared to be flying directly over the family farm. In utter shock, Ree began to hear the thunderous sound of exploding bombs followed by ugly black plumes of smoke—all in the vicinity of her home. Her eyes locked on the growing plume of smoke.

"Oh, no...not my home!" Ree screamed.

She tore off her shoes and ran barefoot the last few miles to her home.

It was near noon when the exhausted Ree reached

the farm's border. A high, overgrown row of hedges blocked the view of the Gong farmhouse. Breathlessly rounding the corner, Ree skidded to a stop and gawked at the flames and rubble of what was once her beautiful home.

"Sons of mongrel dogs!" Ree shrieked. "I will kill every Jap in the world! How could anyone be so vicious?" Tears streamed down her cheeks. "My home was no threat to them! Why?"

"Miss Gong, welcome home."

Ree froze as she heard the voice from behind her—a voice she had hoped she would never hear again. Slowly, she looked over her shoulder. Standing a scant distance away was Sergeant Suzuki.

Chapter 9

Ree ran head-on at Suzuki, leaping onto the stocky man and knocking him backward. She struck repeated blows to his face.

Swiftly, Suzuki's men pulled Ree off of him.

"Miss Gong, you are a great deal of trouble," said Sergeant Suzuki. He held his samurai sword high over his head with both hands. He stood over Ree, ready to strike. The sergeant then lowered his sword and returned it to its scabbard. "What a pleasure to see an old friend once more," Suzuki said, rubbing the bandaged ear Ree had bitten the day before.

"How did you know I would be here?" said Ree, struggling to free herself from the soldiers who held her arms.

Suzuki smiled. "An acquaintance of yours named Tang told me. He had great praise for you. He said you were the member of a very prominent family in the Kiangsu Province. The lovely man was one of several spineless Nationalist soldiers slated for execution, but in exchange for his life he offered to give me information about the beautiful, brave girl who amputated my ear. I had him executed, nonetheless. How can one trust someone who would betray a fellow countryman?"

"Sergeant, if you know everything you would know this farmland belongs to my family. You and these other bastards have no right to be here," Ree said.

Suzuki and his men erupted into uproarious laughter.

"Miss Gong, this good land that your bare feet are standing upon is now the property of the Japanese empire. You and your family are the trespassers—the survivors, I mean," Suzuki finished with a smirk.

Ree's heart jumped into her throat. "Survivors?" she stuttered. "You mean…"

"Yes, young lady. Sadly, those who do not obey orders and give respect to soldiers of the Japanese Imperial Army must pay a heavy toll," Suzuki said, pointing toward a stand of eucalyptus trees at the edge of the melon field. "Come this way, angel face. Come see the price for impoliteness."

A deep anxiety swelled in Ree's soul. She didn't want to move or see what was in the grove. She knew one or more of her family must have been slain by Suzuki and his men, and guessed their bodies were lying there under the trees. But which of her family members did they kill? As they walked the few hundred yards to the grove, she prayed she would not find her sister or mother lying among the eucalyptus leaves. A flash of terrible guilt burned inside her. *One should not wish life for one family member over another,* she thought.

As they neared the stand of trees, Ree reflected on how much joy she had felt as a child playing there with Mi, and how the cool shadows of the immense trees had refreshed them in the heat of the summer. But now those same blissful trees appeared menacing, like hideous demons guarding an ominous secret.

"This way," Suzuki said, threading through the fragrant-smelling trees. Then he stopped. "Look there, angel face. Look closely into the dark shadows." He pointed, guiding her eyes to a clearing in the grove.

Hesitant, Ree looked. She could make out a lifeless figure lying on the cool, damp earth. Stepping cautiously forward, Ree recognized the bloodied, nude body of her kid sister, Mi. Tears welled up in Ree's eyes. She observed another lifeless body bound to the trunk of one of the trees. She felt as though a knife had been plunged into her heart. The second body was that of her grandmother, Mama On.

"Mama On's shoes..." Ree whispered. "Please allow me to remove them. At least her feet can be unbound in death."

"No!" snorted Sergeant Suzuki. "We have no time for such nonsense."

"I will remove your grandmother's shoes," interjected a soldier, drawing a small penknife from his pants pocket.

"Suit yourself," Suzuki said impatiently.

The soldier respectfully removed the dead woman's shoes and cut away the ragged cloth to reveal her disfigured feet.

Ree defiantly broke free to bid farewell to her dead relatives. "Goodbye, Grandmother," Ree whispered, kissing her on the lips. She then approached Mi and dropped to her knees. She cradled the lifeless body of the sister she had argued with so incessantly throughout their brief lives.

"Now you see the consequences when one does not obey the Japanese Imperial Army," Suzuki lectured.

Overwhelmed by the tragedy, Ree could not cry or speak. She kissed her little sister passionately on the lips. Then she laid Mi's body down on the rich soil of their beloved farmland.

Ree rose to her feet and lunged at Suzuki, swinging her fists wildly. The sergeant blocked the young girl's blows. With a single swipe of his hand, he knocked Ree to the ground.

Ree sat up and rubbed the side of her bruised cheek. "Where are my parents? Do they live?" she muttered.

"Stupid, stupid angel face," Suzuki crooned. "Forget your parents. You must think of your own welfare first. Your grandmother and sister insulted me as you have, but unlike them, I forgive you. We will return you to Nanking to be registered and interned. Remember, Miss Gong," he finished philosophically, "the man with the gun makes his own laws."

Ree frowned. "I had a Chinese general tell me the same as you. You're both sons of whores."

"Such language," said the soldier who had removed Mama On's shoes. "Where would a young Chinese girl learn such language?"

"From field hands whenever my parents were not present," spat Ree. She thought it odd that people who raped and killed found foul language offensive.

With bound wrists, Ree was placed into the back of a military truck. During the journey back to Nanking, the brilliant light of midday made the tragedy of the conflict even more evident. Ree saw that many of her beloved winter melons were absent from the fields—no doubt appropriated to feed the hungry Japanese army. The burning ruins of homes were scattered across the countryside, and countless rotting bodies, both human and animal, were strewn alongside the road. The offensive stench of death was already saturating the air.

Suzuki and the other soldiers laughed and boasted of their easy victory over the poorly trained and under-equipped Chinese Nationalists. Ree sat silently during the ride, trying to block out her captors' idle chatter. Her mind dwelt on the reality that she would never see her sister or grandmother again. She swallowed back her tears. As heartbroken as she was, she would not give her captors the satisfaction of seeing her cry.

As they neared the Nanking wall, Ree remembered all too well Song's accurate prediction that the wall would offer little protection against their formidable enemy. In fact, the top of the wall was now providing an ideal platform for the victors to celebrate upon.

"Bastards," Ree blurted as she witnessed their drunken rowdiness. "Why must these monsters rub defeat in our faces?"

Drawing closer, Ree was shocked to see the mangled Chinese bodies that had been pushed off the sixty-foot wall. Some of the dead were naked young women and even female children—all of whom were undoubtedly violated before meeting their tragic ends.

The military truck drove through one of the thirty city gates. Passing to the other side, Ree and her escorts were greeted by festive Japanese soldiers parading about the streets, as well as the soldiers celebrating atop the wall. One soldier ran triumphantly back and forth along the walkway waving an immense Japanese national flag. Some celebrants on the wall threw bottles of saké to the soldiers in the back of the truck carrying Ree. Catching one of the bottles, Suzuki gulped the strong drink with gusto. The drunken sergeant forced the drink upon Ree. Her lip tightened as she refused the wine.

"Drink, you whore," Suzuki demanded, attempting to pry her mouth open.

Choking and coughing, Ree spat the wine in Suzuki's face.

"Horse, you prick," said one of the soldiers. "Do you not have enough women without having to force yourself on this poor girl? Leave her alone."

"Mind your own business, soldier," snarled Suzuki, taking a poorly aimed swing.

The two soldiers began to wrestle on the bed of the truck. Ree cowered into a corner.

The truck arrived at its destination with an abrupt stop, slamming the occupants in the back against the rear of the cab. A young, baby-faced lieutenant barked at them: "Enough horseplay! Stop this foolishness at once! Do you forget that you are soldiers of the Japanese Imperial Army? Pull yourselves together and escort the prisoner to the detention center."

"Yes, sir!" said Suzuki and his soldiers in unison, standing at attention.

Ree stood up and realized she had arrived at the Nanking City Park, which had been converted into a detention camp for Chinese civilian prisoners of war.

"Seiji, take this young lady to the registration line," said Suzuki. He looked at Ree and said, "We will meet again soon, Miss Gong. Good day."

Ree knew that Suzuki was a man true to his word. They would no doubt meet again. But now her only thoughts were that of her parents and Song.

"I promise to live if you will do the same for me..." Ree said softly under her breath to the images of her parents and Song that drifted in and out of her mind.

"Miss Gong, this is the registration line," Seiji said. "You are to stand in line. When you reach the front, a clerk will record your name and a tent will be provided for you in the detention center." He paused, then added, "Miss, I am truly sorry for all the trouble we have caused you and your countrymen, but it is our divine destiny to rule China as well as all of Asia—perhaps much, much more. But, I am still sorry."

Ree gave no reply other than a slight nod of her head.

The day had been long and tragic. Ree had had little rest and no food. She began to feel faint as she stood in the never-ending train of civilians waiting to be registered. After almost an hour, Ree fell to her knees, struggling to avoid passing out. As she fought to keep her eyes open, she felt a sharp pain in the middle of her back. Lying on her side in agony, she could make out a pair of dusty and worn military boots only inches from her face. She slowly raised her head and made out a Japanese soldier towering over her. He did not appear much older than she was.

"Bitch, everyone must stand. No one sits. No one lies down," he said, wielding a metal-tipped bamboo rod.

The pain was unbearable. Ree's face grimaced as she labored to stand.

"Move faster!" commanded the guard, raising the bamboo rod to strike her again.

"No more!" said an elderly, well-dressed man. "Can you not see that this young woman is very fatigued? I will hold her up. You need not concern yourself with her, young man," smiled the Good Samaritan. He helped Ree up off the ground.

"I will hold you to your word, old man. If she falls— even a little—I will shoot you both." The guard tapped his bamboo rod on Ree's head as he spoke.

The old man propped Ree upright while the two of them watched the guard prance down the long line of humanity. Ree thought it odd that the old man offered such kindness toward her, a perfect stranger.

"Miss, put your arm over my shoulder. Try to sleep standing up. That is what my wife and I would do," smiled the old man. "We'd both sleep holding each other up."

Ree managed a weak smile. "Sir, you are so kind. But why is it you stood next to me for so long without speaking?"

"Young miss, I am seventy-seven years old. I have nothing to say to young ladies. I only spoke up when I did because someone had to slay your dragon. Since no one else applied for the job, I wanted to be a hero for a young lady in distress one last time. Parts of me may be limp, but my tongue is still firm," joked the man.

"I thank you, my new friend. It has been a terrible few days. I am Ree."

"Young miss, I am Chan Soo. It has also been a bad few days for me, as well."

"You spoke of your wife. Where is she?"

A sullen look drew across the old man's face. "The soldiers shot her this morning as we stood in line. The sons of bitches demanded Boa's string of pearls. She refused and they shot her. Foolish woman. I told her the pearls were not worth her life. I would buy her a new string. Damn woman. So stubborn, like a gwai lah woman."

"You have my sympathy, sir. You are a good man. We will hold each other up," Ree said, resting her head on the man's shoulder.

The line moved at a snail's pace. Three more hours passed before Chan and Ree reached the registration table.

"State your names and occupations," spoke a stern man sitting behind the table.

"Akira," interjected a young soldier standing behind the seated man. "This lovely young girl will make an excellent comfort girl."

"Dear sir, my name is Chan Soo," the old man said. "I am an important banker from Shanghai, and this is my daughter, Chan Ree. My bank has done much business with Japanese companies and I have Japanese friends in high places. If you dare harm my daughter in the least little way, I will see to it that all of you bastards pay dearly."

The bland-looking man rose from his chair. "Mr. Chan, I have difficulty believing your story. It appears that your prestige could not prevent my men from killing your wife," he said, pulling a string of pearls from his breast pocket and dangling them before the old man.

"I curse you all! You will not rape or kill this young woman as you did my wife!" shouted Chan, leaping over the table with amazing quickness for an old man. With a blinding anger, Chan wrapped his hands around Akira's neck. The soldier fought for his breath and cried out feebly for his comrades to come to his aid.

The struggle ended as quickly as it began. A guard rendered a harsh blow with the butt of his rifle to the back of Chan's head. The old man clutched his head in agony.

Akira was assisted to his feet by the guards. He regained his composure and dusted the grime off his uniform. "You arrogant, ancient Chinaman. To assault a soldier of the Japanese army is a serious offense." He drew his pistol from its holster and chambered a round.

"Wait!" Ree said. "Please do not kill Chan—uh, my

father. Make me a whore if you wish, but please do not harm him. He has already paid you with his wife—my mother." Ree sheltered the old man's body with hers.

The dazed man stroked Ree's hair and the two exchanged smiles. "It is all right. I would enjoy seeing my wife again. Survive the best you can, my daughter," Chan said in a soothing voice.

A guard pulled Ree off the old man. "No more goodbyes," he scowled.

Akira placed his pistol against Chan's temple. An all too familiar act was carried out before Ree's eyes—only this time she knew enough to turn away and cover her ears tightly with her hands before the round was fired into Chan's head. Even with her ears covered, the discharged round from Akira's pistol left a haunting ring in Ree's ears.

"Assign this woman a space in Section C," directed Akira in an unemotional voice.

"Enough!" Ree screeched. "No more!"

As the guards dragged her away, Ree whispered, "Goodbye, my hero."

Chapter 10

Within the internment camp were thousands upon thousands of Chinese civilians, while hundreds of thousands more of Nanking's populous remained to be rounded up. Though many of Nanking's wealthy had left long before the Japanese capture of the city, many— some too stubborn to leave, like the Gongs, or those too sick or too feeble to leave—joined the hodgepodge of common laborers, prostitutes, and whatnot in a nightmare of misery.

Ree was escorted through the endless maze of tents that were nothing more than sheets of inferior canvas held up by wooden poles. They stopped at a corner of the formerly attractive city park.

"Here is your assigned tent. You will receive one ration of rice daily and possibly a few vegetables when available. Oh yes—if you attempt to escape the impoundment," warned the soldier, "you will be dealt with quite severely. Do not wander far from your section."

Ree sat on a cot, dejected, in the ludicrous dwelling.

An aged woman's voice called from outside her tent. "What news do you have of the outside world?"

Ree stuck her head out between the flaps of her tent to see an old couple smiling a warm welcome to the newest arrival.

"Welcome to this lovely place of paradise," the old woman said. "I am Xing, and this old goat is my husband, Choy."

Ree paused for a few moments before replying,

astonished that anyone could act so joyful under such tragic circumstances. She returned a smile to the gracious couple. "Pleased to meet you both. I heard on a radio just before I was captured that the Generalissimo is planning to retake Nanking with a great offensive attack. He will lead the attack personally. Be patient. Our troubles will soon be a memory." Ree knew this was a bold-faced lie, but she wanted to give the couple hope.

"Wonderful," said an excited Xing. "Praise the Generalissimo, Choy. I thought we would die in this awful place." Feeling quite ecstatic upon hearing the false hope of liberation, the frumpy old woman drew a silver flask of brandy concealed in her bra. "Sweet daughter, we really must celebrate our future freedom. You must sample this excellent brandy." The old woman extended the flask to Ree.

"The gwai lahs are not totally without some virtue. They at least make fine liquor!" exclaimed Choy.

"Uh, yes—I suppose a drink would feel good..." Ree stopped in mid-sentence, noticing a brilliant green jade bracelet adorning the woman's left wrist. "Where did you get this bracelet?" Ree demanded, grabbing the woman's arm. "It resembles one that belonged to my mother."

"You're hurting my wrist, young lady!" screamed Xing.

"My apologies, Xing," Ree said, releasing her grip. "Now, answer my question."

"A couple traded the jade bracelet for our daily ration yesterday," Xing stated bluntly. "In fact, the woman did resemble you somewhat, but she was not quite so rude as you are."

"My apologies again, Xing," Ree said. "I never learned politeness and I regret to say that I did not learn patience, either. Tell me where the couple is who gave you the jade before I tear it from you."

"Miss? Miss?" Choy questioned.

"The name is Gong Ree," Ree said sharply.

The old couple grinned.

"Are your parents Chou and Zu?" asked Xing, feeling more amused than angered by the young woman's brass.

"Yes! Yes!" responded an excited Ree.

"Then, young lady, you are in luck. Your parents are alive—at least as of yesterday. But no one ever knows one's status from one day to the next in these times."

"Chou and Zu are the names of the couple who traded the bracelet for our rations," Choy said. "They are somewhere in this detainment camp. But, dear Ree, this prison is truly vast. There must be at least thirty thousand detainees in this impoundment."

Ree hugged the old couple. "The day is young, or at least I am young. I will find them."

"Miss Gong, I hope your parents are alive for your sake. I can't think of anyone else who would enjoy your company," the old woman said facetiously.

For the remainder of the day Ree walked tediously up one row then down another, peering into every tent, often to the disdain of the occupants she startled. She screamed out her parents' names. As darkness fell, Ree's voice had become hoarse and her legs and feet ached. Dejected, she returned to her meager shelter and collapsed onto the floor with exhaustion.

Though very tired, she slept lightly. The constant barrage of voices and footsteps outside her tent denied her a peaceful night's sleep. At dawn Ree forced her sore and stiff body to rise and resume her laborious search for her parents.

The beautiful city park she and her younger sister had once played in had transformed into a festering eyesore. Most of the vibrant green vegetation had been spirited away to provide fuel for the prisoners and invaders alike. Choking smoke saturated the air. Ree covered her mouth and nose with a bit of cloth she tore from her skirt, trying to block out the smoke, as well as the smell from the enormous piles of human excrement and the decomposing bodies of her countrymen and women who had succumbed to torture or outright execution. Around the clock the morose hills of the dead grew higher and higher from truckloads of lifeless citizens that were dumped by the Japanese soldiers.

Ree was oddly detached from the horrors that surrounded her. Perhaps her mind and soul were numbed by the continuous barrage of human suffering around her. She feared she was becoming unfeeling and without conscience, like her tormentors. But her survival, and that of her parents and Song, took precedence over her other feelings. It was unsettling, but whatever guilt she may have had had to be set aside for the time being. Her first priority was to find her parents.

Endlessly, she peered into tent after tent, shouting her parents' names. After hours of fruitless searching, everyone Ree came into contact with began to look alike. Delirious with frustration and fear, she began rummaging through the stacks of rotting corpses, mumbling nonsensically to herself.

A voice that she had heard countless times in anger and disapproval resounded faintly from the front of a long line and drew her attention. Her mind clearing, she walked in the direction of the arguing voices. The line was long and trailed into a zigzag pattern. Taking a circuitous route, she finally reached the front. As Ree had hoped, there stood her father and mother. The proud patriarch was demanding a larger food ration for himself and his wife.

"Father! Mother! You're alive!" screamed Ree, weeping as she approached them with open arms.

Stunned, Zu gawked, speechless, at the sight of her oldest daughter. Then, realizing that Ree was not a ghost, but still very much a body of flesh and blood, Zu ran to meet her daughter. "Ree! Ree, your father and I thought you were dead," she exclaimed with elation.

Ree's father stood stoic, not looking upon his oldest

daughter.

Releasing her mother, Ree walked the few paces to hug her father.

Coldly, Chou brushed Ree aside. "Please, daughter, it is discourteous to show personal affection in public."

Ree withdrew a few paces.

Zu once more wrapped her arms around her daughter and kissed her repeatedly.

Ree glared at her father. "Father, you cannot forgive me for abandoning the family? You have suffered. The family has suffered. But I suffered as much as anyone, my loving father," Ree said.

As the prideful father stared down his oldest daughter, who was guilty of the same stubborn pride, Zu nestled her face against Ree's cheek.

"Ree, do not be angry at your father's cold welcome. Jun is dead. Your brave brother died defending his country. Dead too are Mama On, Mi, and all of our servants. They separated us. We were told later by a Japanese soldier that they were executed. Understand that it is very hard for a man—any man—to express his sorrow," she whispered, her lips so close that Ree could feel her breath against her ear.

"Mother, I saw the bodies of Mama On and my sister. I did not know Jun was dead. We were never close, but I'm proud he died for China. That should count for something," Ree said.

A gaze of morbid curiosity crossed her mother's face. "Daughter, we were informed of Mama On's death and of Mi's...did the Japanese..." She seemed afraid to finish her sentence, but expected Ree to answer nonetheless.

Ree glared at her mother. "Mother!" she said, as if offended by her question. "Do not ask such a foolish question. Do you wish for me to draw you a picture?"

"Enough of this family reunion!" commanded the officer in charge of rationing. "You will receive no ration today."

"You do not know who I am? I am Gong Chou, the most important farmer of winter melons in Kiangsu Province," proclaimed Chou.

The officer displayed a look of mock surprise and embarrassment. "A thousand pardons, Mr. Gong. I had no idea who I was speaking to." He motioned to a subordinate. "Please bring Mr. Gong and his family a triple portion of rations," he commanded, winking at his subordinate.

"It is about time some of you people treated me with the respect I deserve," Chou said smugly.

The subordinate soldier scurried back with a heavy metal pail and placed it at Chou's feet. With puzzlement, Chou gazed into the bucket. To his disgust, he found it filled with horse manure.

"You goddamn bastard! You insult me and you insult my family!" Chou shouted.

"Eat it, Mr. Gong. Eat it now," ordered the officer.

Chou wore a hateful scowl as he lifted the pail. The officer guffawed loudly and his subordinates joined in laughter at Chou's humiliation.

The indignant patriarch held the pail to his lips as if to comply with the officer's demand. But instead of following his orders, he threw the manure over the head of the offensive officer. "I prefer my horse manure cooked," Chou said.

The absurd spectacle caused a torrent of gleeful applause from the Chinese prisoners, who had had little reason to laugh since the invaders' arrival.

The subordinate soldiers began to savagely beat Chou with their metal-tipped bamboo rods. In vain, mother and daughter pleaded with the soldiers to stop the assault. Chou frantically rolled over the ground, his hands covering his face to block the stinging blows. Large welts started to appear on his body.

Their pleas for mercy ignored, Ree leapt onto the back of one of the soldiers. With flailing arms she struck the man's back and head. A fellow soldier attempted to pry the spirited girl off his comrade. Ree succeeded in halting the brutal beating of her father, redirecting the soldiers' wrath upon her.

Before the soldiers could inflict any serious harm, three rounds sounded from a service pistol. The soldiers stopped hitting Ree's helpless body and stood stiffly at attention.

"Stop, you idiots!" said an authoritative voice. "Is this any way to treat our Chinese hosts?"

It was a voice Ree easily recognized. Removing her hands from her face, she saw the man who had caused her and her family so much grief: Sergeant Suzuki.

The ration officer bristled. "Sergeant, what right have you to order my men about? I have the rank of lieutenant and you are only a sergeant! This insolent Chinese prick dumped horse dung on me. You have no right to usurp my authority."

"Lieutenant, you are nothing but a pencil pusher. Why should being doused with horse shit offend you when you are already full of horse shit?" Suzuki replied. "Take this man and woman to the infirmary and make sure their wounds are treated well," he commanded.

"May I go with them?" asked Zu.

"Why yes, of course. It is only proper that family members stay together," Suzuki replied. He looked at Ree. "Take care, Miss Gong. I told you we would meet again…and again…and again…"

Chou and Ree had their wounds treated at the infirmary. Then together the trio returned to the dreary tent city.

Chapter 11

Over the ensuing days the Gong family bore witness to the worst atrocities one culture could inflict upon another. Young girls, old women, nuns, and even men were raped, tortured, and killed. Every day the toll of Chinese slaughtered numbered into the hundreds. Some days, thousands.

Realizing the dire straits the Chinese citizens were in, the consulate and ambassadorships of several countries, as well as the Red Cross, banded together to create a Nanking Safety Zone. It was a virtual sanctuary setup at Nanking's Ginling Women's Arts and Science College. These humanitarians from several nations worked around the clock to save as many Chinese lives as possible. Ironically, despite the Japanese's savage treatment of the Chinese, the Japanese agreed to honor the boundaries of the Safety Zone.

The Gongs' close friends, the British Ambassador Sir Farnsworth and his daughter Sylvia, were among those who joined the concerted effort to save as many people as they could from the flagrant butchery, but most specifically Sylvia and her father wanted to rescue what remained of the Gong family.

Nanking was an immense, sprawling city with thousands in the detention centers and thousands more trying to elude the enemy as best they could. Nevertheless, unaware of the newly created Safety Zone and Farnsworth's efforts to find them, the Gongs sat in their flimsy shelter, totally numbed by the constant atrocities that occurred daily outside their tent.

"We've been here in this hell hole for over a week. Why not do what they wish with us and get it over with?" spoke Ree.

"Dearest daughter," responded Zu, "there are hundreds of thousands of prisoners in Nanking. Our turn will come soon enough."

"Sylvia and her father will help us. I know they will, if we can just hold on until they find us," Ree stated, trying to give hope to her parents, but not knowing whether the Farnsworths intended to help them or not.

Chou replied with a dejected shake of his head. "My foolish daughter, do you really believe a gwai lah would bother with the plight of a non gwai lah? Any non gwai lah?" he said, his words mouthed weakly as a result of hunger and desperation.

Zu observed with almost a sad what if, "Dear husband, we would not be in this unfortunate situation to begin with were it not for your silly pride. Sir Farnsworth offered us shelter and protection from the Japanese invaders, and you shunned him because you could not bear the thought of anyone but Gong Chou, the fearless patriarch, being the family protector. You were ashamed that you could not protect us. Now look where we are."

Chou slapped his wife's cheek. "I have protected my family ever since my father died!"

Zu spit blood out of her mouth and wiped the tears from her face. "Like you protected your mother and your youngest daughter? Like you drove away our only son? He got himself killed as a result. He could not live up to your expectations," cried Zu.

"Whore! I am the richest farmer in Kiangsu Province. I am not weak. I did not want these bad things to happen to my family, but it was unavoidable. When the devil intruders come for us, I will die bravely without complaint. In return, I will ask them to spare the miserable, worthless lives of my wife and only surviving child."

Trying to ease the tension between her parents, Ree stepped between them. "Please, Father. We're all a little crazy in these foul times. We've lost a great deal. The Japanese hurt you badly, but do not do the same to your wife—my mother."

"There you go again, my daughter, with that brash mouth of yours," replied Chou. "Jun is gone. I have no reason to live, anyway," stated Chou, lying down on his cot.

"What a heartless bastard. You speak of your dearest son, but you speak no words of grief for the loss of our youngest daughter, and no words of concern for Ree, who still lives," Zu scolded.

Chou rolled his eyes in an uncaring manner.

"Forget it, Mother. Father's only love is for a child that has a dangling root between its legs," Ree said dejectedly.

Chou shook his head. "The female soul I do not understand. I was rich enough that I could have easily taken a second wife had I wished. But I did not out of respect for you, Zu. Hear me out: Women are indeed less valuable than men simply because we are needed to work the fields to provide food and clothes for those who do little but bear children."

Ree and Zu stared at the Gong patriarch with disbelief.

"Father, you can't be serious. I work the fields with you, by your side," Ree said scornfully.

"Yes, I know, my daughter. What a pity you do not have a penis—or perhaps you do possess one and I just didn't notice," Chou mocked.

"You arrogant—"

"Everyone out of the tent! Now!" commanded Sergeant Suzuki, stopping Zu in mid-sentence.

"Bastard!" cried Ree. "We were having a family conversation!"

"Such a strong-willed young woman," said Suzuki. "What a shame, Miss Gong, that you are not Japanese. The three of you will come with us."

"Where are you taking us?" Zu inquired.

"You are to be servants of the noble empire of Japan in payment for liberating China from the yoke of gai jin," Suzuki replied.

"Lies," Ree blurted.

"Such a sharp tongue for someone with an angel face," Suzuki said.

Ree knew the spiteful and sadistic sergeant had a horrific fate in store for her and her parents. And she knew there was little, if anything, she could do about it.

Perhaps there will be peace and harmony for us in another life, she thought as they were escorted to an unknown destination.

Ree wondered if her parents knew that their family home had been completely obliterated, since they made no mention of it to her. In any case, her own survival and that of her parents was the most urgent issue.

While being transported through the streets of Nanking, the three Gongs were ordered not to speak and to sit passively. The once bustling, boisterous metropolitan city was now void of pedestrians and auto traffic, with the exception of marching Japanese soldiers and military vehicles.

Like in the detention camp, the countless bodies of Chinese citizens were piled high, later to be disposed of in the Yangtze River. All over the city buildings burned. Those that weren't burning were damaged by artillery shells. All too often the vehicle the Gongs rode in had to swerve around a bloated body in the street or around a shell crater.

After several blocks of ghoulish scenes around her, Ree shut her eyes and began thinking of Song, her winter melons, Mama On, Peking Duck, and anything else she could bring to mind that would distract her from the morbidity around her. When the vehicle finally stopped, Ree opened her eyes to see that she was at the base of the city wall.

The three prisoners ascended the sixty-foot wall with Suzuki and two other soldiers. The Gongs felt the sting of Suzuki's bamboo rod when their pace was not quick enough to suit him.

"An eye for an eye...or is it a head for an eye?" Suzuki said, rubbing what remained of the ear Ree had bitten off.

"Enough toying with us," Chou exclaimed. "You want to kill us? Finish it now and be done with it."

Suzuki smiled, pacing around his three captives, eyeing them as a butcher would eye a prime piece of meat. Father, mother and daughter stood stoically, side by side. Although they were afraid of whatever the Japanese sergeant had in store for them, they would not give him the satisfaction of showing their fear.

"My friends, no one has to die, or even sacrifice an ear. As I've so stated, you will serve the empire loyally. At least the two Gong women, that is. As for Mr. Gong, I am not certain of what service you can be to the empire, but I promise you that you will most certainly live, provided you do this one small favor for the empire and for me." Suzuki grinned. "All that is required of you in order to live is to copulate with your daughter."

The proud patriarch stared at Suzuki with total contempt. "You can't be serious."

"Very much so. You must have sex with your daughter to live," Suzuki repeated.

"And will I see my home again?" Chou asked.

"You have no home. It was a casualty of war."

Chou and Zu looked at each other with stunned shock.

"Father, Mother, I was not sure if you knew about the loss of our home. I was afraid to ask," said Ree. "Such evil people. It is not enough that you butcher my grandmother, violate my sister then butcher her, and kill my brother—you also took away the only home I ever knew!" Ree screamed.

Suzuki and the other soldiers laughed uproariously.

"Fools. Yes, we took the lives of your relatives, plus many more in the line of duty. But we did not bomb your precious home. You may thank your protector and savior Generalissimo Chiang Kai-shek for that particular sin," Suzuki pointed out. "Your Generalissimo ordered the destruction of many province homes and other structures that might benefit the devil Japs."

"Bastard. The Generalissimo had no right to do that," said Ree.

"But what is done is done," lamented Suzuki. "At least three members of the Gong family remain alive. But for how long? You must be pragmatic and do whatever is necessary to remain alive. Mr. Gong, pleasure your daughter, now!" he demanded.

"Wait!" Ree said. "Please—I took a piece of your ear in anger. I apologize. You possess a very sharp sword. I beg you—take my ear and spare my father this humility." Ree pulled her long black hair away from her right ear.

A thin smile crossed Suzuki's face. "A generous offer, Miss Gong, but you will be of less service to me and my country minus an ear." He turned to Chou and drew out his samurai sword. "Now, Mr. Gong, do as I request, or I will separate your head from your body."

Zu dropped to her knees and began to sob, pleading with Suzuki to stop.

The proud patriarch glared at the sergeant defiantly. "No, I will not have sex with my daughter. Not even to save my life. You've taken everything from me, but I will at least keep my dignity. You can take nothing else from me."

"Husband," Zu said in a shaky voice. "I am your wife and your oldest daughter lives. How can you say you have nothing but left to lose?"

Chou glanced shamefully down at his feet. "Yes, I also stand to lose a wife and my only surviving child. It is difficult, dear wife. We lived so many years together in the same house but yet seldom spoke of anything of substance." A thin smile crossed the patriarch's face and he reached his hand out to his wife and only surviving child. "The words were not there, and I am so sorry, my wife and number-one daughter. I had to bear the yoke of being a man."

Chou took one last glance at his wife and daughter. Then the overly-proud winter melon farmer stepped off the city wall, falling to his death, and denying Suzuki the satisfaction of further humiliating Chou, or beheading him.

Zu and Ree cried out sorrowfully. They dared not look down to the street at Chou's broken body. They dropped to their knees and embraced each other.

"What a shame," Suzuki commented cruelly. "I would have enjoyed watching father and daughter pleasuring each other. Now, enough time mourning. You will now allow me to escort you to the Royal Jade Hotel. I believe it is the finest hotel in Nanking. It now houses the officers of the Japanese Imperial army. You both shall have the honor of being comfort women for these brave men. Of course, I will need to sample the two of you first to be assured that I am offering my officers a quality product."

Ree released her embrace with her mother and stood up defiantly. She spit in Suzuki's face. "Sergeant Horse Suzuki, I will kill you someday. This I promise you," Ree scowled.

Suzuki smiled, wiping the saliva from his face. "My ancestors were fearless samurai. I look forward to the day you try."

Arm in arm, mother and daughter descended the wall to board a truck bound for the Royal Jade Hotel.

Chapter 12

"Mother," Ree asked as the vehicle raced through the desolate streets. "Isn't the Royal Jade the place you and father were married?"

Zu held Ree's hand. Grinning and weeping simultaneously, she reflected on how strange it was that she was not to meet her groom until their wedding day. Like any bride, she had been nervous and apprehensive. Sharing memories she had never shared before, Zu went on to tell Ree how handsome Chou had been and that he assured her that he would keep her and their future children safe and happy. Zu then went cold, silent, not sharing with Ree that her years with Chou would turn out to be empty and unfulfilling. Though her husband of more than twenty years was not especially cruel or abusive, he was nonetheless self-absorbed and fearful of displaying any open emotion toward his wife and children.

I was nothing more than a babysitter and a housekeeper, Zu mused to herself. *But at least Chou's parents gave me an elegant and festive wedding reception.*

"Mother, mother...we're nearly at the hotel," Ree said, tapping her mother's shoulder. "What will they do to us?" Ree hoped to gain some comfort from her mother.

"Ree, my daughter, you are young and strong. You can overcome anything. You were never afraid to speak your thoughts—something I was never able to do. We must hold on to our lives, no matter what. Do not forget your father died for you."

"What horse dung, Mother," Ree replied. "I wish I

could believe that Father died to protect my pride, but I don't. I believe he walked off the wall to save his own pride."

"Ladies, we have arrived!" proclaimed Suzuki. "Today is the day of your redemption."

"This hotel was so beautiful," Ree said. "You bastards violated our buildings as well as the people of China."

Mother and daughter were escorted into the hotel lobby. Once inside they were confronted by a whirlwind of chaotic activity. Japanese soldiers streamed into the hotel while a multitude of other soldiers exited the building. Chinese prisoners, mostly young women, paraded about under the watchful eyes of armed guards.

A smug attendant grinned at them from behind the desk. "Fresh fish! Finally, you bring me Chinese women whose faces do not frighten the dead. They will be good morale boosters for the men."

"Saito, I will be the first to get my beak wet," Suzuki said. "Place mother and daughter in neighboring rooms."

"Take your lady friends to rooms 701 and 702," muttered Saito.

Zu and Ree were dragged to an elevator, which took them to the seventh floor.

"Be strong, my daughter," whispered Zu as they ascended to the seventh floor.

The elevator doors opened to a rush of screams and cries emitting from behind the doors of the hallway rooms.

"Hold on to Mother Zu while I prepare my angel face for her service to the empire," ordered Suzuki to his men.

In desperation, Ree struggled gallantly with her captor, but Suzuki was much stronger than she was. Her glancing blows did little harm to his hardened body. The men pulled the brash young woman off their sergeant and restrained her.

"Take me, but do not harm my mother, I beg you," Ree pleaded.

Zu stood whimpering, too emotional to speak.

Her arms twisted behind her back, Suzuki shoved Ree into the hotel suite and slammed the door behind them. "Be nice, Miss Gong. Cooperate and your mother will not be touched, I promise," Suzuki assured in a bold-faced lie. He motioned for the young woman to undress.

Ree believed the sergeant's words. She stripped, and without further resistance, as ordered, and reclined upon the fine goose-down bed. Suzuki tied her to the brass posts and left to attend to Zu.

Bound naked to the bed, Ree was blind with fear. But her fears were more for her mother's welfare rather than her own. She knew Zu possessed a far more delicate nature than she did. If the Japanese soldiers raped and abused Zu, her body might live, but her soul would not. Ree could only pray Suzuki would be true to his word.

Strangely, like the lull before a great storm, Ree felt somewhat at peace temporarily as the ceiling fan caressed her bare skin and the silk sheets soothed her bruised and tired body.

Ree's thoughts shifted to Song, the only man she had kissed. She prayed he still lived and was out of harm's way. She had hoped Song would have been her first man. She attempted to find humor amidst the tragedy as she mused that Song would now have to wait in line like all the others yet to come.

For the next two days Ree and Zu were raped and abused by Suzuki and countless other Japanese soldiers. Given such brutality, many could not survive such treatment, physically or emotionally, but Ree was a woman of strong will and driven by the hatred for the man she felt was responsible for all of her losses and misery: Sergeant Suzuki Toro. Zu also clung to life, but the Japanese had stolen her soul, just as Ree had feared.

As the third day of torment was about to begin,

mother and daughter had given up all hope, having resolved themselves to the fact that only blessed death would end their suffering.

Chapter 13

On that third morning, a loud pounding on the door of Ree's room interrupted Sergeant Suzuki's sadistic activities.

"I asked not to be disturbed!" Suzuki shouted to the interloper.

"This is Sir Justin Farnsworth, the British Ambassador," came the irritated reply. "I am accompanied by my daughter, Sylvia, and your commander, Major Marita. We order you to open this door at once or I shall break it down!"

The startled sergeant pulled on his pants and scrambled to open the door. He flung it open so forcefully that a loud bang rumbled throughout the hallways. Half-dressed, the nervous sergeant stood at attention and saluted his commander.

"You bloody bastard. If I were not a representative of the British government, I would beat you to within an inch of your life. Instead, I must present you these papers, releasing your prisoners Gong Ree and Zu into my custody. You must stand down, sergeant."

As the ambassador cursed Suzuki, Sylvia rushed to Ree, tears flowing down her cheeks as she untied her and spoke with comforting words.

Major Marita shook his head. "Sergeant Suzuki, you are a disgrace to your uniform. Sir Farnsworth, my apologies. Understand that not all Japanese soldiers are like this man. My nation does not have a monopoly on unprincipled, immoral men."

"No doubt," replied the ambassador. "I have seen my

own nation rape much of the entire world. I sometimes question what God had in mind when He created man."

"Yes, Mr. Ambassador, the world is ugly. Sadly, many of my superiors are looking the other way as monsters like Suzuki commit these terrible sins. Are we the only sane people remaining?" mused Major Marita.

"I pray not," replied Farnsworth.

Once Ree was free of her restraints, Sylvia approached Suzuki, who remained in a rigid stance. She glanced at her dear friend's naked, battered body. Then she turned and looked at Suzuki with burning eyes. She struck him across his left cheek. "You hideous monster! You insult all of mankind by simply breathing."

Suzuki was seething. "Young woman, you dare strike a soldier of the Japanese Imperial Army? You insolent gai jin. You will pay for this effrontery."

"Sergeant Suzuki," the major said, "Lady Farnsworth will answer to no one—certainly not you. The young lady has diplomatic immunity, as does her father. You shame me. You shame your emperor. Leave, this instant."

"Yes, sir," growled Suzuki. He saluted, gathered his remaining clothes, and departed.

Semi-conscious, though unable to speak, Ree gave her rescuers a pained smile.

The ambassador and his daughter gingerly wrapped Ree's bloodied body in blankets, then rescued her mother in the adjoining room. They drove them to Ginling University. Behind the arbitrary boundary line Ree and her mother, along with thousands of other Chinese, would be safe from the merciless enemy. Once the news spread of the sanctuary, thousands upon thousands of Chinese fled into it in desperation. The Japanese continued to brutalize and massacre those unfortunate enough not to reach the Zone.

Unlike most of the Nanking citizenry, who took great risk entering the Zone, Ree and Zu were chauffeured inside without incident by Sir Farnsworth and Sylvia, protected by diplomatic immunity. Once within the sanctuary, the two Farnsworths took Ree and Zu to the makeshift infirmary set up in the university gymnasium. Both mother and daughter were semi-conscious as Red Cross workers and volunteers from various embassies worked frantically to save their lives.

Night and day Sylvia stayed at their bedsides, praying for the speedy recovery of her cherished friends. Meanwhile, Sylvia's father drove the streets of Nanking daily, spiriting away as many Chinese citizens as his Phantom Rolls Royce could hold. Under the scornful eyes of the Japanese soldiers, he would deliver them to the Nanking Safety Zone shielded by his diplomatic status.

The number of refugees in the Safety Zone swelled to the breaking point. Working with little rest and around the clock, Red Cross workers and members of the Foreign Diplomatic Service risked their own health and well-being to feed and shelter the growing population within the boundaries of the sanctuary. When the workload became too overbearing for the medical volunteers, Sylvia took over the care of Ree and Zu. Gradually, with her committed attendance, the two women regained their health. The physical wounds healed, but the wounds to their souls would require far more time.

After a month of convalescence, mother and daughter were up and about, and able to tend to their own needs. Having close ties to the British Ambassador, Ree and Zu were assigned to a private room in a building formerly used as a university dormitory. This was a true luxury, given the scarcity of housing space for the Chinese refugees. Many had to sleep in hallways or in the open air on the Ginling University grounds.

Winter was now approaching. The days grew shorter and the morning air grew crisp. Despite the decreasing temperatures, Zu spent her days sitting on the balcony of their living quarters, neither speaking nor displaying any emotion. Whatever gaiety and spirit she once possessed had been stolen from her by Sergeant Suzuki Toro and his fellow soldiers.

Ree had fared only slightly better. She fell into a deep depression after being told by Sylvia that she would never be able to bear children. Some days Ree would curl up in her bed naked, with the bed sheets covering her head. Often she would not rise until late afternoon.

Their only visitor was Sylvia, who came every afternoon to bring them food from the embassy kitchen. Ree and Zu would only eat a small portion. Sylvia would say to both women, "Please, you must eat to regain your strength." To Ree she would say, "Your mummy will not even come in from the balcony to chat with me, and like you, she refuses to eat."

Ree stared with empty eyes at the food that was turning cold. "I must find Song. Help me find Song. He will be safe here," she muttered.

Sylvia gazed at her friend, shocked at her request. "My sister, I would do anything for you. I would even give my life to save you. I do wish your gentleman friend could be with you in the Safety Zone, but it is simply out of the question. Only Chinese civilians are allowed in the Safety Zone. Chinese servicemen are not."

"I couldn't care less about silly damn rules!" Ree shouted. "We must find him. I have no one else."

Sylvia slipped into bed beside Ree and wrapped her arms around her friend tightly. "Ree, you are my sister— in spirit if not by blood—but you can be very silly at times. Your mother is sitting on the balcony no more than ten paces away, and she is very much breathing; I am most certainly breathing, as well. You are not alone."

Ree sat up in her bed and brushed her flowing hair away from her eyes. She began to massage her forehead to revive her groggy mind. "My mother may move about and breathe, but she is not living. She has not spoken a dozen words since our rescue."

"Your mother is in pain, as you are," responded Sylvia. "It is a deep, invisible pain that will take some time to heal. You must be patient with your mother. I care for you a great deal," Sylvia finished. She leaned forward and gave Ree a gentle kiss.

Ree smiled. "Sylvia, we are so close. You saved my life and that of my mother, but I need Song. He touches my soul like no other. Please help me find him."

Sylvia pushed her friend away. "Damn you! Goddamn you! If I had a penis I would fight Song for your affections. Come. I will drive you to the prison camp that was set up to house the Chinese soldiers. Possibly your loved one will be there. I warn you, though, that the Japanese consider it a dishonor for a soldier to be taken alive. A true soldier and a true man dies fighting. Therefore, they're butchering hundreds of Chinese soldiers daily, so do not hope for much, my sister."

Ree looked bewildered at her childhood friend's revelation. "Sylvia, my beloved friend, I did not realize you cared for me in this way. We kissed and touched each other's private places, but we were only children exploring our bodies and what it felt like to kiss another person." Ree placed her hand lovingly against her friend's cheek. "I'm confused about our relationship... girlfriend?" said Ree, leaping from her bed with renewed energy.

"Girlfriend, let's go find your boyfriend," Sylvia said in a dejected voice.

The girls borrowed an embassy car, and Sylvia drove Ree across town to the detention camp for Chinese soldiers. The camp was even more appalling than the one designated for the civilians. The two women looked with horror at a row of human heads, lined up like coconuts, sitting on the prison grounds.

"I cannot bear to look," Ree said, trembling and closing her eyes tightly. "Do you see Song's head, Sylvia?"

"Their faces are distorted. I cannot say for certain if he is among them," Sylvia replied.

The car sat idling once they stopped at the entrance to the camp.

"Hold on, my sister, be strong," Sylvia advised as one of the guards approached the vehicle. She faced him and said flatly, "Guard, I am Lady Sylvia Farnsworth. My father is the British Ambassador and this is my assistant, Gong Ree. I wish to speak to a prisoner named Lt. Song Tai."

"No," replied the guard coldly. "It is forbidden for anyone to speak to the prisoners."

"Bloomin' idiot. My father is Sir Justin Farnsworth, and I repeat: He is the British Ambassador to China. My father is not the kind of man you wish to anger, and I will personally attend your ritual *seppuku* if you do not cooperate."

The guard reeled back with fear and embarrassment. "My sincerest apologies, Lady Farnsworth. Uh, of course...let me see..." He shuffled through the log of prisoners interned in the camp. "Yes, you are in luck. We do have a prisoner named Lieutenant Song. It appears he has dysentery and is located in the restricted area for the ill," he said, now eager to please. "Here is a pass to allow you and your assistant back out. You will have need of it because I will being going off shift and there will be new guards manning the gate. Good day, Lady Farnsworth," he finished with a smile.

Following the guard's directions, Ree and Sylvia drove to a separated area fenced off from the main campground. The restricted area was not much different than the primary grounds, except for housing the seriously ill and severely injured. The women stopped directly in front of the entrance, stepped out of the car, and entered a long, tented structure. The overwhelming stench of death and human waste attacked their senses. They saw a handful of Red Cross nurses and doctors frantically treating the sick and wounded who were sprawled upon filthy blankets on the hard ground.

"Please, Miss, can you tell me the whereabouts of a Lieutenant Song?" Ree asked a nurse.

"Such a waste, such a waste," the nurse muttered to herself, oblivious to Ree's question. "We work so hard to save them only so they can be executed by the Japanese or die because we do not have enough medicine and facilities to treat them."

Exasperated, Ree tapped the nurse on the shoulder. "Nurse, I'm talking to you."

The preoccupied woman almost jumped out of her skin. "Lady! Can't you see that I'm busy? I have no time for chit-chat."

"Nurse, I too put in long hours at the Nanking Safety Zone," Sylvia said, clearly agitated. "My girlfriend is a victim of the Japanese invaders. We did not come here to discuss the weather. Just tell us where the prisoner named Song is and you can return to saving the world."

"Do forgive me, dear women. I forget that others sacrifice and give their all in these difficult times," said the nurse. "You will find your man over there. He is the third man from the left." She pointed to a row of prisoner patients to her right.

Sylvia kept her distance while Ree approached the groggy, emaciated man. The nurse must have been mistaken, Ree thought. But she then recognized Song's soft brown eyes, which still sparkled when he looked at her. His thick mane of black hair had thinned, but still had lovely waves in places.

"Ree? Ree…I feared you were dead," uttered a faint, familiar voice. "I should have guessed a woman of your strength and courage could not die easily."

Ree grinned. "You mean a woman who is too bitchy and stubborn to die?" she said. She dropped to her knees and took a hold of Song's hand. "I didn't recognize you at first. You're out of uniform," she mused. "I was not sure you remained alive. I will nurse you back to good health. There are too many things left undone for us," Ree said, stroking Song's gaunt face.

"No, it is too late. The Japanese have stolen everything I have. I have nothing left. I wish I had something to give you," Song said.

"You have already given me more than any other man has given me. You cannot leave me, Song. The invaders have already taken so much from me: my father, brother, my sister, my grandmother. If that were not enough, the bastards turned my mother into a shadow. They've stolen my soul."

"My apologies, my beloved Ree. You've lost so much, but I am dying."

"Please, dear lieutenant, don't go. You've forgotten our agreement to meet atop the wall and finish our tea," Ree reminded him, her eyes swelling with tears.

Sylvia moved to within a few feet of Ree and Song. "Ree, time grows short. We must leave now. We are not even supposed to be here."

Ree looked at Sylvia, and in a low voice mouthed: "We must take Song with us to the Safety Zone or he will die in this wretched shit hole."

Sylvia displayed a thinly disguised look of exasperation. "Ree," she barked. "Have you not heard one word I've said? Chinese soldiers are not allowed. Only civilians may enter the Safety Zone."

"We can at least try," Ree said. "Take off your trench coat. I have need of it," she requested politely.

Sylvia was reluctant, but did as she was asked. "You are mad, my sister. Your gentleman friend could not love or desire you as much as your English sister."

Ree grasped Sylvia's hand and pressed her face within an inch of Sylvia's ear so that no one else could hear her words. "Sylvia, I know you care for me, and I you. But there are places I think Song can take me that you cannot. I beg you—please help me."

Sylvia murmured through a quiet chuckle, "My Chinese sister, we are too much alike to be lovers. Take the damn coat."

While the Red Cross workers were distracted by their overwhelming workload, the two women placed the trench coat on Song's frail body. Supporting him, Ree and Sylvia placed him in the car and drove to the guarded gate.

"Song, my love, you must sit straight and be alert. It will be over soon," encouraged Ree.

"Stop!" ordered the guard, stepping in front of the car as it rolled up to him.

"Let us pass. I am Sylvia Farnsworth, the daughter of the British Ambassador. The young Chinese woman is my assistant, and this gentleman is a Red Cross worker. He is not well, which should be no surprise. Who would not become ill working in this cesspool?" She thrust the pass into his hand. "Here, take this. It is the pass given to me by the guard who manned the gate before you."

Skeptical, the guard read the scribbled note. "Why does this man look so ill? He appears sicker than his patients. You gai jins think all Asians are fools. I should have you two bitches arrested for aiding a Chinese prisoner in escaping!" he shouted, angered by the obvious deception.

"Arrest my noble ass? You will do nothing of the sort," Sylvia replied brashly. "I have diplomatic immunity."

"Very well, you and your assistant are free to leave, but this Chinese scum will stay. He must be punished for his crime of attempted escape," replied the guard.

"If Song stays, I stay," cried Ree.

Sylvia exclaimed, "Soldier, I refuse to believe all Japanese soldiers are monsters. Surely there must be one among you who does not have a heart of stone." She pointed to Song. "Can you not see that this man is gravely ill? He is my assistant's husband. He is no threat to your great empire. Have mercy and allow him to die in a clean, warm bed with his wife beside him."

The guard contemplated Sylvia's plea. "Ladies, I command you two to leave here at once, and take your Chinese prick with you," he said, trying to be more menacing than he really was.

Sylvia pressed her foot down on the gas pedal. She then slammed on the brakes after moving only a few yards. She got out of the car and walked back to the guard, put her arms around him, and placed a peck on the stunned soldier's cheek. "I was right. There is at least one good man in the Japanese Army."

Blushing, the guard gently rubbed the spot on his cheek where Sylvia planted her kiss. "Such strange people, the gai jin," he reflected as he watched the shiny black Rolls Royce disappear into the distance.

Chapter 14

The trio made their way back to the Safety Zone, but they knew they had one more hurdle to cross. Sylvia stopped the car a few blocks from the gate. Together the two women assisted Song into the trunk. Ree placed a good luck kiss on his lips before closing the trunk lid.

Taking full advantage of her status as the daughter of the British Ambassador, the trio easily passed through the guarded entrance to the Safety Zone, avoiding the usual vehicle inspection.

Song, with the foolish pride of a young man and military officer, was embarrassed that he needed the care and protection of two women. With the elevator not working, he insisted upon walking, unaided, up the six flights of steps to Ree's room. With a strong determination, and in complete agony, the young soldier struggled up the stairs with Ree and Sylvia following close behind, ready to catch him should he fall. After many long, excruciating minutes, they finally reached the dorm room.

Sylvia kicked open the door. Out of sheer exhaustion, Song swallowed his pride and braced his arms over the shoulders of the two women. Together they took him to a firm bed and placed him on it.

Zu was sitting on the balcony. She heard the commotion and peered through the curtain to see a man reclining on Ree's bed wearing a tattered military uniform. Her mind was no longer grounded in reality. It made no difference that he was out of uniform, that he was Chinese rather than Japanese, or that he was obviously in very poor health. All she saw was a man—the image of those who stole her possessions, her loved ones, and her very being.

"Get out! Get out!" she screamed. "You cannot have me again. No more! No more!"

"Mama, this man is not a Japanese soldier," explained Ree, trying to calm her hysterical mother. "Do you not remember Lieutenant Song? He came to court me. He too was victimized by the invaders."

Zu rolled up into a fetal position. She would not hear her daughter's words of reason.

Sylvia placed a sympathetic hand on Ree's shoulder. "Your poor mother will be forever bound to a bed being abused by Japanese soldiers. Clearly she cannot stay here with Song. I will take Zu to live with me at the British embassy. Father and I will take good care of her. I promise."

Ree took Sylvia's hand and kissed it lovingly. "You are truly a dear friend, Sylvia," she said.

Zu was unwilling to budge from her invisible hiding place on the balcony. Sylvia summoned two Red Cross workers to assist her in transporting Zu to the embassy. Ree watched her mother's removal with mixed feelings, torn between her obligation to her mother and her love for Song.

Once Ree and Song were alone, Ree drew a hot bath for him. As the steamy water filled the porcelain tub, Ree undressed the man she desired so much. Like an infant, Song sat without emotion as his clothes were removed. His mind and soul were seemingly elsewhere. Like Zu, he sought a dark, hidden place where he could be free of any further pain or loss.

Ree noticed signs of torture over much of Song's body as she gently lowered him into the tub.

Song grabbed her arm and said, "Did the invaders have their way with you?"

"Excuse me?" Ree said, startled.

"They raped me. Did that Suzuki do as much to you?" blurted Song again with a blank stare and unemotional voice. "They did things to me as they would a woman."

Ree excused her lover's blunt manner, knowing he was not himself. She fished for Song's right hand in the soapy water and pressed it to her cheek. "We've had so many bad things happen to us, dear Tai, life can only get better. The past is past. We will be in a better place someday. You have my word on it."

Song stared at their reflection in the full-length mirror that stood a few feet from the tub. He displayed little response to Ree's words of reassurance. He snatched the sponge from her hand and threw it at the mirror. "Bastards. I'm going to Japan to personally kill the emperor for his crimes against China, but not before I kill Sergeant Suzuki. He came to the prison to boast of what he had done to you, how he had made love to the daughters of Gong Chou, the richest farmer in Kiangsu Province. I lunged for him, but the guards struck me down. Then they hung me upside down and beat me with bamboo rods until I passed out." Song's words were spoken in a strange, unfeeling voice.

"Oh, my love, I am sorry for what they did to you, but we must move on. You are all I have left."

"Your family was killed by the intruders?"

"All except my mother. You saw her earlier. Yes, they were murdered by the Japanese. All except my father, who died in a different way."

"What way?"

"He...he walked off the city wall to his death when Sergeant Suzuki ordered him to have sex with me," Ree choked.

"Suzuki alone will forever be a parasite attached to my soul. I had hoped Suzuki was only making an idle brag about making love to you and your sister, but you didn't respond to my question, so I will take your silence as a yes."

Ree looked down at the sudsy water, feeling shame with the knowledge that the man she loved knew she had been with another man, albeit against her will. "My beloved Tai, when the time is right for us, we will sleep together and it will be beautiful. Forget Sergeant Suzuki. He is not worth our attention," she said, leaning over to kiss Song's forehead.

"It is too late, Ree. I wanted so much for the both of us."

"No, it is not too late. We're both young, and..."

A knock on the door interrupted her.

"Who is it?"

"A messenger from the British Embassy. I was instructed by Lady Farnsworth to deliver some clothing to a Miss Ree," came a voice from the hallway.

"How wonderful," Ree said as she rushed to the door. "Sylvia has sent some of her father's clothes for you, Song. You'll be looking like a proper English gentleman in no time."

A young Chinese boy stood in the doorway holding two bags of finely tailored men's clothing. As the boy handed the clothes to Ree, an odd look crossed his face. The boy looked over Ree's shoulder and dropped the bags of clothes onto the floor.

Ree spun around to look behind her. With a gasp of horror, she saw Song on the balcony, naked and dripping with bathwater and soap suds. He leaned against the railing precariously.

"Your father chose a pleasant way to die," he said to Ree. "You are my only love, Ree, but it is too late. Goodbye, my love."

Song blew Ree a kiss, then slipped over the railing, plunging to his death.

Chapter 15

"Song!" Ree shouted. "No!"

She rushed to the balcony's edge, praying her lover was alive, but knowing he could not survive such a fall. Far below, Song's mangled and bloodied body resembled that of her father's, who had jumped from a similar height.

Ree was near hysterics. Song's death seemed unfathomable to the young woman who had seen and experienced so much tragedy in such a brief period of time.

Ree straddled the railing, wanting to be with Song—if not in this life, then in some other. She released her hold from the railing. She could feel the subtle whiff of air as she began to fall. Then suddenly she was jerked back, as if some divine hand had intervened in her desperate act. Her head struck the iron railing. Dazed, small bursts of colored lights danced before her eyes. As her mind and vision cleared, she could make out her savior. It was the young messenger boy, who had grabbed her in midair and was now struggling to carry her to the bed.

"Let me die," cried Ree. "You had no right to do this."

With great difficulty, the Good Samaritan managed to place Ree upon her bed. Ree, being a strong, athletic woman, was beginning to gain the upper hand over the slight boy when two Red Cross workers entered the room to investigate the commotion. Much to the boy's relief, the two men aided him in subduing Ree.

Word of the mishap soon reached the British

Embassy. In a frenzied rush, Sylvia arrived within the hour and raced up the stairs. Panting for air when she reached Ree's room, Sylvia flung the door open. To her dismay, she found Ree bound to the bed for her own safety. Beside her sat the protective teenaged messenger boy. Sylvia hugged her friend and placed a lingering kiss on her forehead. "It is so divine that you live, my precious friend," she whispered to Ree.

Sylvia drew a thick wad of money from her purse. She handed the sum to the messenger boy. "Boy, I am in great debt to you. You are now free to leave. I will tend to Miss Gong's needs from here on."

Once the boy left, the two women stared at each other, neither quite sure what to say. After a long silence, Sylvia, noticing that Ree's wrists and ankles were rubbed raw and bleeding, said, "Ree, you've hurt yourself. Allow me to bandage you."

With a scornful look Ree began to pull and kick at her restraints. "Get these ropes off me! I was tied to a bed before. I swore it would never happen to me again!"

"It was for your own good," Sylvia said in a motherly manner. "You wanted to join Song. I will not allow it. It is too soon for you to spend an eternity with him."

"Damn you," said Ree, continuing to struggle. "You only want me for yourself."

Sylvia threw a hurtful look at Ree. "Yes, you mean so much to me and it is selfish of me to want you to live. Song could not defeat his demons, but, my lovely friend, I thought you had enough courage to conquer yours." She pulled a penknife from her purse and severed Ree's restraints.

Once Ree was free, Sylvia stood up and motioned to her, beckoning her toward the balcony. "Ree, I love you more than my own life. Come. We will join your precious Song if you have grown tired of living."

Slowly, Ree struggled to stand. Face to face with Sylvia, Ree was deeply touched by her girlfriend's gesture. Ree grinned. "You would step off the balcony with me?"

"Walk with me to the balcony edge and we will see if I am sincere," Sylvia replied with an equally enigmatic grin.

They held hands and walked out onto the balcony. The two young women stared down at the macabre blood stain left by Song's body. Sylvia removed her shoes to make her climb over the railing easier. With their hands locked together, the pair leaned against the railing.

"Ree, my love, I hope we do not land on our faces. I want us to be beautiful, even in death," mused Sylvia.

Ree rested her head on Sylvia's shoulder. "Damn gwai lah, you will be the death of me," she giggled. She stepped back from the railing. Sylvia had made her realize it was not yet her time to die.

"But not today, dear sister," replied Sylvia, stroking Ree's hair.

"Dear gwai lah, you have saved my life for the second time, but what kind of life do I have to look forward to? I have lost everything, and my mother's mind and soul was stolen. How can I help her when I cannot even help myself?"

"My sister, come back inside and I will fix us both a cup of tea. I have something monumental to tell you."

After preparing the tea, Sylvia sat beside Ree on the sofa. She handed a cup of hot tea to her cherished friend. She held out her own cup to offer a toast.

"Sylvia, you do not put milk and sugar in your tea like so many other English people I have known. You are becoming very yellow. What are we toasting?"

"To your future. To our future. Given the perilous times now existing in China, Father has been called back to Mother England. I am returning with him."

Ree was so taken aback by her friend's announcement that she accidentally spilled hot tea on her lap. "Damn you. Damn you! You save my life only to abandon me and my mother? You gwai lah bitch! I hate you!" Ree cursed.

Sylvia smiled. "It takes a bitch to know a bitch. Indeed, I may be a bitch, but I do not abandon my friends. I want you to come with me. England is very beautiful this time of year. Before this terrible madness came to China, you were able to show me all the loveliness of your country. At least the beauty of Kiangsu Province. Now, please allow me to show you my country." Sylvia was almost giddy with excitement.

Ree looked at her friend with apprehension. "I've never been outside of Kiangsu Province, let alone China, and what of my mother? What is to become of her?"

"Father is still in possession of the Yank stock your father gave him to hold. The sale of those stocks should be enough to place your mother, at least for the time being, in one of the fine establishments in England that care for troubled people like her."

Ree glared at Sylvia. "That gwai lah stock was meant for Jun, and this fine establishment you speak of, it is no less for people who have lost their minds, people that are crazy or unwanted, like an old pair of shoes you no longer want. You wish me to place my mother in a dark corner of the closet to be forgotten?"

"Your mother needs a great deal of care. You yourself admitted you cannot care for her alone. You may visit her whenever you wish. It is not like you are casting her aside," Sylvia said defensively. "Your brother Jun is no longer with you. In fact, all the Gongs have gone to their proper rewards, except for you and your mother. Like so many men, your father was too embarrassed to state that he loved all his children, not just the one with an appendage between his legs. Sister, come to England with Father and I. Life will be better for you and your mother. It could not be any worse. The Japanese grow stronger in China every day. Please accept," pleaded Sylvia. She planted a loving kiss on Ree's lips.

As if having to drink bitter tea, Ree reluctantly agreed to Sylvia's offer and accepted her late father's assets.

Ree had Song buried in the family plot. She placed a flower on his grave and the graves of her family members. She mouthed words to all of them that someday she would return. Mother Zu sat in a wheelchair sullenly at the grave of her husband, Chou, completely unaware of her surroundings.

Ree and her mother boarded a chartered plane, along with Sir Farnsworth and Sylvia. The plane lifted off the runway and circled Nanking to gain altitude. China's provisional capital looked so different from above. So much fear gripped Ree. Nanking, the city of her birth, was the only large city she had ever known. She knew nothing of the world beyond the borders of Kiangsu Province. But she knew there was no other choice for her as she squinted her eyes to see through the morning haze. She saw the massive internment camp and archaic city wall that stood helplessly against a modern, mechanized army. She could make out the never-ending lines of humanity, waiting for what scraps of food the enemy would allow them, trying to fend off death for another day.

Sadly, the plane did not fly over the Gong farm. Ree reflected upon what a good harvest of winter melons it would have been that year. So many things raced through her mind; but the clearest image that cut into her soul was the face of Sergeant Suzuki. It seemed as if all the evil in the world had been implanted into the body and spirit of that one man. Though she had promised to kill him, Ree hoped she would never see him again. She had been through so much, and had never been one to back away from anything in her life, but she could not bear to see the man who had been the cause of so much misery to her and her family.

After a long journey, the plane finally landed in

London. The all-too-frequent English fog had rolled in, and the cold dampness felt like a slap on the face to Ree, who was used to the dry, warmer climate of her homeland.

Ree rode with the others to London in a finely polished Rolls Royce, not unlike the one Ambassador Farnsworth rode in while residing in Nanking. As they neared the Farnsworth's townhouse, the fog began to lift, exposing the hectic pulse of a large, metropolitan city. The sights and sounds of London were so much more intimidating than the somewhat smaller Nanking, which Ree had always thought to be a large and great city.

As they rolled up to the front entrance of the ambassador's home, Ree felt nearly breathless as she looked at the imposing structure that stood before her. Ree's family home was considered to be one of the finest residences in all of Kiangsu, yet it would have appeared insignificant placed beside the Farnsworth dwelling. Ree was indeed now living in a very alien world.

Ree said a sad farewell to her mother, who spoke no words or displayed any expression as the Farnsworth chauffeur drove her to the asylum on the outskirts of London. In her own mind, Ree kept repeating to herself that she had been brutally raped, beaten, and had come close to death more than once. If she survived such suffering, then surely she could survive in the lo fon world.

Chapter 16

After a brief period of adjustment to the English weather and gwai lah customs, Ree would pass her days planting and tending a small vegetable garden in the well-manicured townhouse rose garden—much to the chagrin of the ambassador, for she had dug up some of his prized roses. She would often tend to the garden barefoot, like a commoner. To Ambassador Farnsworth's further dismay, daughter Sylvia would join Ree on occasion, also barefoot, to assist her with the garden. Although Sir Farnsworth was disappointed that Ree did not attempt something more elevated, such as getting an education, he admired the young Chinese woman's fortitude and strength after the hardships she had endured in homeland China.

"Anyone who can grow vegetables of any kind in such an ill-suited place like England deserves my admiration," Sir Farnsworth reflected.

But despite her friendship with Sylvia and her days in her vegetable garden, which reminded her of a time when she grew winter melons with her family, there was still an unfulfilled yearning within her—a feeling of not belonging. The ambassador and Sylvia tried their best to make Ree feel comfortable in their world. They took Ree to concerts and plays, and numerous social functions. But Ree felt she was beginning to lose the part of herself that she called Chinese. She did not want to be yellow on the outside and white on the inside, and that was what she feared she was becoming.

Over the passing months Sylvia and Ree began to

drift apart. Sylvia, who was beautiful, with pearl-toned skin and blonde hair, was engrossed in gala dances and the constant attention of both young men and women. Though Ree herself was also an attractive young woman, she felt she was being patronized and mocked behind her back by Sylvia's circle of lo fon friends. The love Sylvia expressed toward Ree in both words and actions in China appeared to have faded with her return to the land of gwai lahs.

One early morning as Ree went out to tend her garden, the groundskeeper casually mentioned to her the existence of London's Chinatown. It was an enclave of the immense city she had not been aware of. This information invigorated Ree, who had been sullen and withdrawn for some time. Once again she would be able to be among the people who looked like her and spoke the same tongue.

That night after the ambassador and Sylvia retired to bed, Ree quietly left the townhouse without notice to anyone that she was going out for the night. She took a taxi to cross the city to a seedy section of London. To Ree's disappointment, Chinatown, like most Chinatowns throughout the world, was nothing more than a ghetto with a glorified, exotic title.

Because she was young and female, the Chinese residents of London's Chinatown eyed her suspiciously. Men, both gwai lah and Chinese, approached her, offering money in exchange for sex. Ree cursed them in Chinese. Ironically, some of the lustful Chinese spoke with heavy English accents and had long ago forgotten their native tongue. Ree's feeling of depression and betrayal was even more consuming than ever before.

Ree wandered the streets of Chinatown, which looked nothing like the real China. Gaudy, flickering business lights accented an elderly Chinese woman who stood vigil in front of her establishment.

"Nui doy," she called. "You are lost. Please come in.

We will drink tea together. Perhaps you would join me and eat winter melon soup with me?" she asked politely between puffs from a thick cigar she chomped on.

"I have not eaten winter melon soup since I left China," Ree replied. "I would be so honored to join you. Does your soup also have big black mushrooms? It would not be good without them."

"Of course, winter melon soup would not be winter melon soup without them," agreed the old woman.

Ree entered the old woman's business while observing a sign above the door: Madam Woo's Fine Dining Café and Bar. Ree thought it odd that there were no customers in the dining room. Sitting at one of the tables, the old woman shouted in a graveled voice to an unseen employee in the kitchen. A moment later, an old woman waddled slowly out of the kitchen, balancing a large soup tureen, two bowls, and a bottle of liquor on a large tray.

"I am Madam Woo. Now, my beautiful nui doy, who are you?" asked the old woman. She began ladling generous portions of steaming broth and chunks of winter melon into Ree's bowl.

"I am Ree. I am from Nanking. I have only been in gwai lah land less than a year," Ree said nervously between swallows of the hot soup. "Winter melon is so excellent..." Ree began to cry.

The matronly woman quickly poured from a liquor bottle and handed a glass to Ree.

"What is this?" Ree sobbed.

"It is the finest brandy in all London. Do not fret, Missy. It is only natural you should miss your land of origin. These are troubled times. I have heard of the cruel things the Japanese bastards did to my fellow countrymen in Nanking. Now another evil demon in Germany wishes to do cruel things to my adopted country, as well. I can only pray the Germans do not attempt to violate you and I, as I've heard the Japanese did in Nanking," Madam Woo said, gulping down her own glass of brandy.

Ree began to feel less despondent and afraid with the combination of the strong liquor and the old woman's comforting words.

"Come, Miss Ree. Come with me to my secret place in the back of my restaurant. There you can lose your worries. You can lose yourself and forget for a time what a miserable world it is we live in." Madam Woo smiled widely, revealing her teeth, which were made entirely of solid gold dentures.

Ree wanted to forget her loneliness and the ever-widening abyss that was growing between her and her one and only true friend, Sylvia Farnsworth.

They rose from the table and walked to the back of the restaurant. Madam Woo took hold of Ree's hand and opened a door, which resembled the door to any inconspicuous closet. From behind the insulated door rushed the loud din of more than a hundred Chinese men and women playing various games of chance. Ree easily recognized the mah jong and the pai gow games that her father used to play. She remembered the game of pai gow fondly, having played it often with sister Mi and Grandmother On.

Ree stepped into the smoke-filled room where she was greeted warmly by the various gamblers, most of a low income status. Like Ree, the players had a deep sense of not belonging to a world where any non lo fon was cast to the shadows of society to be ignored or taken advantage of. Ree did not feel totally at ease with Madam Woo's customers, but her former life was gone forever, and like Madam Woo's regulars, the gambling parlor presented a joyful diversion from an otherwise mundane, uninspiring, and alienated existence.

Ree lost what money she had carried with her that night, so Madam Woo loaned her a small sum for the cab fare home. Although Ree had lost, it marked the beginning of nightly visits to Madam Woo's gambling parlor. Gradually, Ree's gambling consumed her, and with each visit to the parlor she would lose more and more money. As Madam Woo had so eloquently informed Ree, she could easily lose herself in that establishment. The games of chance and the brandy would not defeat Ree's demons, but at least she could hold them at bay.

In time, Sir Farnsworth and Sylvia grew deeply concerned with Ree's depleting inheritance and drinking problem. Like brother Jun, Ree would often spend her daylight hours confined to her bedroom in a drunken stupor with the curtains holding back the offending sunlight. Ree's vegetable garden was now withered and yellow from neglect.

After a period of several months, Sylvia could no longer tolerate her friend's irresponsible behavior. Early one morning she barged into Ree's dark bedroom and flung the curtains back, flooding the room with bright morning sunlight.

"Ree, my beloved sister, you are wasting your life. You came home at five this morning. There was a time when you used to rise at that hour to work your melon fields," Sylvia scolded. "You were raped and you lost your home and family. So, now you feel sorry for yourself? Would you have preferred it was I who was raped? Get on with your bloody life. For presently, your shoddy life is as worthless as the huge pits of night soil we saw at the detention centers in Nanking."

Ree rose and sat on the edge of her bed, shaking the sleep off and rubbing her eyes. She pulled back her bedraggled hair. With her eyes half open, Ree looked toward Sylvia, who stood over her, waiting for a response. "As a matter of fact, yes," Ree said.

"Yes, what?"

"Yes I would have preferred it was you that was raped so I could lecture you, as my grandmother used to lecture me for swearing and going barefoot in the house,"

Ree chuckled.

Sylvia sat on the bed and placed her arm around Ree. "And like your grandmother, I criticize you because you're a stubborn, silly girl. Your money is dwindling fast. I did not want to tell you this, but my father has been paying for your mother's care for some time now."

Ree turned her head away from her friend in shame. "I'll pay your father back, even if I must sell my body in Soho."

Sylvia struck her friend across the cheek. "Ol' gal, you're too skinny to be a prostitute. Understand, it is not the money my father and I want from you. It is your salvation. I know you, remember? You need an obsession. For much of your life it was your precious winter melons. The obsession you have now is eating your soul, just as that horrible Suzuki tore your heart out."

"My gwai lah sister, what do you suggest?" replied Ree, realizing for the first time just how destructive her gambling and drinking addiction had become.

"Sister, do not laugh, but I have been going to a weekly art class. Some weeks they have such lovely female models with such divine breasts, and sometimes male models with such enormous organs." Sylvia giggled. "Remember the lovely drawings you used to draw when we were children?"

Ree shook her head, grinning, knowing Sylvia was correct, that her life needed direction. She rolled her eyes at her friend's preposterous suggestion. "Song's body and soul was the only man I was interested in, and as for women's bodies, I am not yet ready to go there."

"But, my lovely sister, painting is a pleasant diversion, far less harmful than what you are doing now. Forget what I said of the nude models. Think about the reward of painting itself." Sylvia cast her eyes to one side in deep thought. "I have an idea. Learn to paint a portrait of Suzuki, and then together we will burn it. Together we can bury at least this one demon. Please?"

Sylvia begged.

"My gwai lah, I have no talent," Ree said.

"My Chinese sister, you could not be more wrong."

Ree didn't respond after a long pause. In frustration, Sylvia left the room, not knowing if her friend would indeed attend art classes, or if her lecture about Ree's self-destruction had touched her friend in any way.

Two days later as Sylvia walked to a Rolls Royce waiting to take her to art class, she was pleasantly surprised to find Ree sitting in the back seat. Ree seemed far more relaxed and refreshed than when they had last spoken.

True to Sylvia's words, Ree found painting to be a far more rewarding way to pass the time than her all-night drinking and gambling binges. Ree was clearly a natural talent, and soon became the darling of the class. Moreover, she painted a large canvas of the man she had killed in her mind daily: Sergeant Suzuki Toro. Oddly, the portrait seemed almost benevolent rather than evil.

Taking the portrait back to the townhouse, the women carried it to Ree's bedroom. Resting it against the wall, Ree and Sylvia sat side by side on the bed, observing the painting.

"Bravo, well done, my sister. I congratulate you," said Sylvia.

As if she didn't hear Sylvia's compliment, Ree stared, as if mesmerized by the portrait. She had hated Suzuki so intensely...perhaps it was time to move on, she thought.

Sylvia placed her arm over Ree's shoulder, kissing her on the lips.

"My gwai lah sister, this is the first time you've kissed me since we left China," whispered Ree.

Sylvia pressed her body against Ree's. "My yellow sister, I ignored you out of spite because I was jealous of your fondness for Lieutenant Song. I will not mince words. I'm in love with you. Let me take care of you.

Forget Suzuki, forget China. Together we'll burn the painting of the monster."

"I'm beginning to love you, my gwai lah sister," said Ree under her breath. She planted a kiss of her own on Sylvia's mouth.

"What is this rubbish!" shouted Sir Farnsworth. The bedroom door, which had been ajar, allowing him to see inside, was flung open.

"Father, I...I..." Sylvia stuttered.

"Miss Gong, how could you betray me? I treated you like my second daughter. Now, I have no daughters of any sort. What you two are doing is a sin against God!" Sir Farnsworth stomped away.

Sylvia ran after her father, begging his forgiveness. "Please, Father, why must love only be exclusive between a man and a woman?"

Sir Farnsworth brushed her aside and walked away. Sylvia dropped to her knees, sobbing.

"I'm sorry, Sylvia. Perhaps it is a sin to the gwai lah god," Ree said, kneeling beside Sylvia and embracing her.

"Ree, my lover, first we must kill the demon that haunts you. I will then reason with Father. He will understand. He must understand. I love you too much to let you go," Sylvia said, wiping the tears from her cheeks.

The two women loaded the Suzuki portrait into the Rolls Royce and drove out into the English countryside. They stopped along the banks of a quiet chalk stream and leaned Suzuki's portrait against a large bolder. Sylvia retrieved a bottle of 20-year-old scotch from the car. Removing the cork, she and Ree each gulped long swallows of the liquor. Sylvia then doused the paining with the rest of the bottle. Ree struck a match.

"At least symbolically you will kill the man who has taken everything from you," Sylvia said.

Before Ree could set the portrait aflame, an unexpected distraction arose. Eyeing the sky south toward London, the two women saw and heard what they had hoped they would never see or hear again. Resembling the V-formations of wild geese and the steady drone of bees, numerous war planes flew directly over London. Both women knew all too well what that meant. Soon, like thunder rumbling, the roar of exploding bombs and clouds of black smoke began to rise from the city.

"Bloody awful Germans!" Sylvia cried. "Why?"

Concerned for Sylvia's father's safety, the women leaped into the car and raced back to London, leaving Suzuki's portrait sitting beside the slow moving stream.

Chapter 17

Ree and Sylvia sped into London. Both shared the sense that their failure to burn the painting represented an ominous message of tragedies yet to come. They reached the inner city and were confronted with a mirror image of the mad turmoil that had taken place during the Japanese invasion of Nanking. Each city street presented a chaotic congestion of humanity, all trying to flee the city or go underground into the subway system. Traffic slowed to a crawl. Growing impatient, Ree and Sylvia left the Rolls in the middle of the street and ran the last half-mile to the Farnsworth's townhouse. As they neared the row of expensive homes, acrid smoke began to engulf them. Blinded, Ree and Sylvia held hands and forged ahead.

The screams and shouts of firemen acted as a beacon for the women as they walked blindly in the direction of Sylvia's home. Close to panic, Ree and Sylvia were suddenly blessed with a strong breeze. To their amazement, they discovered that they had been standing in front of the Farnsworth townhouse for several minutes—or rather, what was left of it.

Irrationally, Sylvia attempted to run into the burning rubble. "Father! Father!" she cried.

Ree tackled Sylvia, pulling her back from the intense heat. "Sylvia, the fire is too hot. Nothing could still be alive in there."

Regaining her composure, Sylvia huddled with Ree. The two women stared wide-eyed at the once magnificent Victorian home. Neither cried. Having already been through so much in Nanking, it was as though they had no more tears to shed.

"Sylvia, I am so sorry," Ree whispered. "We've been through so much. You caught me when I fell in Nanking, and you caught me again in London. Now I will catch you if you fall. Be brave, my gwai lah sister."

"Ree, you are my lover and my very best friend. We will catch each other," Sylvia said, kissing Ree on the lips. "Father! Where is Father? I would willingly sacrifice my home in exchange for my father's life," Sylvia cried.

"Lady Farnsworth?" inquired a soot-covered fireman.

"Yes, I am Sylvia Farnsworth."

Despite the man's blackened face, one could see the sorrow etched into his eyes. "Dear lady, I regret I must inform you that your father has gone to God."

Speechless, Ree and Sylvia held each other tightly.

"The poor gentleman came to what was left of his home. He shouted your name and that of someone named Ree. No doubt he thought the two of you were still inside. I tried to stop him, but the dear man pushed me down. He then ran into the burning building. A wall collapsed atop the poor soul, crushing him to death. You may take comfort, young miss, that your dad died quickly. I do not think he suffered much. Undoubtedly, his last thoughts were of you. My deepest apologies, Lady Farnsworth," the fireman finished, placing a comforting hand on Sylvia's shoulder.

Sylvia fought back her tears. "So much loss. Those goddamned Krauts. I can now understand why you have so much anger toward the Japanese, Ree."

Finally, the tears did come. Ree began to weep heavily. "I told myself you would not see me cry. Men do not cry. I am only a weak girl."

A sad grin crossed Sylvia's face. "Funny, I told myself the same thing. I did not want you to see me cry," she said with tears streaming down her face. "Father and I never had the opportunity to make amends. I wanted him to understand how much you meant to me. My father died no longer loving me."

"Your father ran into a burning house for us...for *you*. This he would not have done if he did not still love you," said Ree.

"Father, I wish we could have reconciled; now it's too late," Sylvia whispered.

The two women sat together on the curb that fronted the former Farnsworth home. Like everyone in London, the girls were shocked by the devastation brought by the German bombings. But such destruction only marked the beginning of many months of almost daily, then nightly bombing raids by the Germans. Fearing for her own safety and that of Ree's, Sylvia booked the earliest flight to New York City for them both. Ree had a great trepidation toward being uprooted again and leaving her mother behind, but Sylvia convinced her beloved friend that the two of them had little recourse but to leave England. Ree had already lived through the nightmare of the Nanking invasion, and she would not take any pleasure should the Germans invade the British Isles. Moreover, Sylvia assured Ree that her mother would be well taken care of and that all her expenses would be paid. She further added that the Germans would most likely not wish to harm a frail and mentally ill old woman.

Ree said her goodbyes to her mother. As usual, Mother Zu showed no response. She stared blankly at the wall as her only surviving child left the asylum bound for the Gold Mountain. Ree was completely overwrought by her mother's lethargic state of being. She felt a deep sense of guilt, feeling that she was abandoning her mother, but there were few alternatives, if any, as Sylvia had already pointed out.

Given the serious nature of the situation, Sylvia had little time to give her father a proper burial, instead choosing to have him cremated. Then, in a rather macabre gesture, she had her father's ashes placed in an airtight urn, which she carried aboard the plane, keeping it safe by her side as if her deceased father were a fellow passenger.

Among numerous pieces of baggage, Ree had crated several of her paintings, which had been stored at the art school. They carried deep sentiment and she refused to leave them behind. The flight to America was only the second flight Ree had ever been on, and the sight of an endless ocean during the long flight made her even more despairing and apprehensive than she had been on the first flight. The two friends spoke few words during their long journey as they both tried to fight their demons.

The announcement came that they would soon arrive in New York. As they approached the airport, Sylvia took hold of the urn which sat on the empty seat beside her, cradling the container as the plane readied for landing. Ree looked out her window. In the distance, she could make out the faint image of the Statue of Liberty.

"The Gold Mountain," Ree said under her breath. "America. It does not appear to be made of gold to me. Even the statue does not look like it is made of gold. Well, at least I no longer have to deal with the London fog."

After going through customs, the women were whisked away in two taxis—one for the girls and another to carry their baggage. Their destination was the well-known hotel, the Waldorf-Astoria.

Reaching the heart of the great city, Ree was awestruck by the high buildings, so high one could barely see the tops of them. Ree had felt so intimidated when she first laid eyes on London, but this eye-fowl was even more impressive.

"Gim Sam, dear sister," Sylvia chuckled. "I once visited New York City when I was little. The buildings looked so big I cried, thinking they might fall on me."

Ree forced a smile.

The taxis rolled up to the elegant hotel, and a doorman in a gaudy uniform rushed to open the taxi door for the girls. Ree did not trust anyone to carry her crated paintings to their hotel suite. She wrestled one of the crates away from an eager bellboy. She awkwardly carried the crated paintings into the lobby. Sylvia remained outside, assembling the pieces of luggage.

"Idiot China woman!" came a voice from the lobby. "All packages brought into the Waldorf must enter through the servants' entrance."

Ree turned to see a rotund desk clerk who had mistaken her for a delivery girl.

"Get that crate out of here!" he continued. "Dumb chink!"

Ree began to curse the desk clerk in Chinese.

The agitated clerk took hold of one of the crates, attempting to snatch it from Ree's grasp.

"Gwai lah bastard! Take your hands off my paintings!" Ree screamed.

In their heated struggle, both Ree and the desk clerk lost control of the crate. It went flying across the lobby, breaking open and spilling Ree's paintings across the finely polished marble floor.

"Chinese bitch!" shouted the clerk. "You will pay for any damages to the marble floor. I'm call'n some of New York's finest. They'll find ah skinny Oriental floating in the East River if you don't watch that smart ass mouth of yours."

Ree ignored the man's ranting as she gathered her paintings. The desk clerk stepped on her hand and pressed it against the marble floor with his foot.

"Ahhh!" Ree cried out.

"Señor, take your foot off the señorita before I kick your damn ass so hard, El Gordo, you will not land until you reach New Jersey," ordered an obese Hispanic man.

The equally rotund clerk gazed up at the offending voice. His look of annoyance quickly turned to one of humility. "Mr. Rivera, I...I'm just do'n my job. I, uh, didn't mean nuthin' by it. Miss, ya okay?" He scrambled to help Ree up from the floor.

"Señor, if my husband does not kick you hard enough to land you in New Jersey, then I will kick you the rest of the way," said a petite Hispanic woman standing next to Mr. Rivera.

"Señora Kahlo," groveled the clerk. "Sorry, I didn't know this China girl was a friend of yours."

"She isn't, gringo. Get out of our sight. Now!" exclaimed the Hispanic woman.

Ree stared at her rescuers with disbelief as well as appreciation. "Thank you for helping me," she said to the couple. "I did not think lo fons living on the Gold Mountain would be so kind."

The Hispanic couple laughed as they helped Ree gather her paintings.

"We behave so civilized because we are not gringos. We are from Mexico," laughed the woman. "What magnificent paintings."

Ree gazed at the couple inquisitively. *What an odd couple,* she thought. The man was enormous, and the woman so small and fragile looking. And why did the woman's eyebrows connect in the middle? And what of her moustache? Why didn't she shave it off?

The couple examined Ree's paintings one by one with careful scrutiny.

"Miss, your paintings are outstanding," said the woman. "They mirror pain, loss, suffering...they grab the viewer's attention by the balls and don't let go. Your name?"

"Uh, Gong Ree...I mean, Ree Gong. It is a Chinese custom to use first name last, last name first."

"Excellent," replied the woman. "Your paintings are reminiscent of the Norwegian artist Edward Munch. The ghost-like faces speak to me."

The man chuckled. "Forgive my wife, Miss Ree. She

is very frank. She does not mince words to be polite." He lifted a card from his wallet. "Please keep in touch. You are far too talented and beautiful a woman to meet only once," he said with a cheerful wink.

Ree was dumbfounded by the bizarre event in the lobby, and even more so by the Hispanic couple that helped her. As the couple entered the elevator, Ree cried out, "Thank you! Are the two of you artists?"

"According to some we are," the woman shouted back.

"Sons of bitches according to others," added the man.

"Buenos dias," said the woman as the elevator doors closed.

"Ree!" Sylvia said. "My God, they liked your paintings. How divine!"

"Who was that grossly fat man and his little wife with a moustache?" Ree asked.

"Sister, that gross fat man and his dwarfed wife are Diego Rivera and Frida Kahlo. Rivera is the most famous Mexican artist in the world. His wife Frida is of equal or even superior talent, but less famous, undoubtedly because she is a woman," Sylvia said gleefully. "You are fortunate to have met such great artists. Who knows, perhaps they will help you climb the Gold Mountain."

Ree responded with a thin, apathetic grin. She had met a few celebrities in her life, such as Chiang Kai-shek and his wife, but Ree was not the kind of person to be overly impressed by fame or fortune. "It is understandable that Miss Kahlo would be forced to live in her husband's shadow, considering his size," Ree remarked wryly, thinking the couple resembled escapees from a circus sideshow rather than famous artists.

Once the women had settled into their adjoining suites, Ree became obsessed with her art, painting late into the night. She also took up drinking again.

Ree had all but forgotten the eccentric Hispanic couple who had come to her rescue, until one afternoon, while passing the hotel newsstand, she spied the headline "Mexican Artist Fired." Below was the buffoonish face of the very same man she had met on her first day in New York. Ree eagerly snatched a copy of the paper and began reading the article. It stated that the highly acclaimed Mexican muralist Diego Rivera had been fired from a commissioned work by an industrialist named Nelson Rockefeller for refusing to remove the face of a Russian communist known as Vladimir Lenin from his mural.

"The funny man *is* an artist, Sylvia was not lying," Ree said aloud.

"Miss, he is also quite the ladies' man from what I hear," blurted the newspaper vendor, noticing Ree's keen interest in the article.

"He's an ogre. Why would anyone but a single-browed woman desire such a man?" questioned Ree.

"Women the world over love men who are famous for something. Diego Rivera is no exception, miss," the paper vendor answered.

"They bed his fame," reflected Ree, handing the vendor the cost of the paper, plus a substantial tip.

The article about the controversial Mexican artist truly piqued Ree's interest. Ree cared little about gaining favor with the famous couple, but art and painting were now her consuming passions. She was anxious to explore new ideas and styles in art.

Casting the paper aside, Ree hurriedly left the hotel, requesting that the doorman flag her a taxi to take her to Rockefeller Center.

Chapter 18

When she arrived at Rockefeller Center, Ree paid attention to the large ice skating rink and the gilded statue adorning one side of it. She was preoccupied with learning more about Rivera—what was it about his art that the gwai lah Rockefeller would want to fire him? She walked to the entrance of the tall building beside the ice skating rink.

"We're closed, miss, go away," said a security guard, peering out at Ree through the glass door

"Please, sir, I wish to see the Rivera mural," begged Ree, pressing her face against the glass, hoping to catch a glimpse of the mural.

"Goddamn it, woman. The building is being renovated. Do you have a Coney Island dog jammed in your ears? I told you to go away."

Ree could vaguely make out men covering the debated mural with white paint. Emboldened by five measures of scotch, Ree rashly pulled a rock from a nearby fountain and hurled the stone through the glass door, scattering shards of glass everywhere. Two security guards promptly grabbed Ree's arms.

"No one is fool enough to damage anything belonging to Mr. Rockefeller, but I suppose yah slit-eyes ain't got the sense God gave white folks. You're going to jail for a long time, miss," said one guard.

"Release my friend at once, you capitalist puppets!" shot a booming voice.

Ree and the guards turned to see a great hulk of a man squirming his way through the damaged door.

"Mr. Rivera, this woman has vandalized Rockefeller property. She must be detained and arrested for her crime," said one guard.

Rivera chuckled. "The Rockefellers have screwed the common man for generations. I do not think one glass door will balance the books. Send me the bill for the damages," he said, stuffing a hundred dollar bill into the pocket of each guard. "So, my attractive Chinese señorita, we meet again. I am very good at saving damsels in distress. Incidentally, why did you not call me? Most ladies do call when I ask them to."

The guards released their grip on Ree and walked away.

Ree did not respond immediately, perplexed by how someone so oafish could be a notorious lover. Rivera took her hand and led her over the broken glass and into the building.

"Mr. Rivera, I think you are a fat clown," Ree stated candidly. "That is why I did not call."

Rivera's immense stomach rippled as he laughed. "Miss Gong, you are so much like my beautiful Frida. She is also an outspoken bitch, but I find it preferable to insincere flattery."

They entered the large anteroom of the Rockefeller Center. Ree was instantly drawn to the nearly finished mural adorning the enormous wall facing the entrance. Using long-handled rollers, men dressed in white overalls were rapidly covering the impressive mural with white paint. Still, Ree could make out a good portion of the mural that had yet to be covered.

It was a multi-faceted montage of the common laborers, and off to one corner one could make out the relatively small face of the communist, Lenin. Though Ree did not particularly like Rivera, she was rather impressed and inspired by his mural.

"What bastards to destroy such a great piece of art," Ree whispered.

"My sentiments exactly," agreed Rivera. "Unfortunately, people would rather obey money than the truth," he reflected as he placed his arm over Ree's shoulder.

Though a tall woman, Ree looked minuscule standing next to the taller, much heavier Rivera.

"Damn the Rockefellers," stated Rivera.

"Who is this Lenin the rich gwai lah Rockefeller dislikes so much?" queried Ree.

Rivera's large stomach quivered as he chuckled. "Ree, my friend, Vladimir Lenin is only the greatest man of the twentieth century. He fought for the rights of peons. Yes, young lady, I am rich, but unlike the Rockefellers of the world, I did not obtain my wealth by exploiting the poor."

Ree gazed into his eyes. "Mr. Rivera, you take money from the rich, people who you say take advantage of the poor. I do not understand."

Rivera laughed heartily. "Foolish girl, you are too young to understand the ways of the world. In a way, I am exploiting the rich gringos by taking their money. My young friend, like my beloved Frida, your paintings express an honest voice that all the world should know. I will make you famous and the whole world will love you." He kissed Ree on the lips.

"Please do not kiss me," Ree said. "The newspaper said you are a world famous artist. The world does not revolve around the great Diego Rivera, though you appear to be large enough to have a planet rotate around you."

Rivera grinned. "You are so much like Frida. I will make arrangements for your first one-woman show at the New York gallery which represents me."

Ree shoved the man aside. "No, there will be no show. My paintings are for me and me only."

"Frida's words, exactly. When I first met her, she said her paintings were too personal to show to anyone. But people need to see the world from fresh eyes. Let the masses share your pain, and of course, rich capitalists will pay you ridiculous sums of money for your paintings so they can pretend that they have a conscience."

Ree rolled her eyes and began to walk away. "My paintings were not meant to be wall decorations in some rich man's house. The world will survive without my art."

"Please stay," Rivera pleaded. "My creation is being destroyed. I do not wish to see one of my children die alone." He took an engraved flask of tequila from the pocket of his overalls. "My anchor Frida would be here to commiserate with me, but her back is acting up again as a result of a trolley car accident years ago."

Feeling that she at least owed some small debt to Rivera, Ree nodded and agreed to stay. Rivera placed two canvas folding chairs side by side, and together the Mexican man and Chinese woman sat together, watching his mural disappear forever.

"Goodbye, Comrade Lenin," spoke Rivera under his breath as workers painted over the image of Lenin. Rivera turned to Ree as the last of his mural was erased with white paint. "Señorita, I thank you for sharing my loss. I sense you have lost more than I. Did you lose your lover to another?"

Ree swallowed another good measure of tequila. "No, my lover did not leave me for another. I lost him in a different way, as I lost most of my family and everything that was important to me. Thieves in the night stole them from me."

"When you say thieves, do you mean the Japanese war mongers who exploit their own race, like the gringo capitalist who has exploited my people for generations? They raped you, did they not? Just as the gringo capitalists have done to the common man the world over."

Having consumed the contents of the first flask, and feeling the effects of his tequila, Rivera spouted in a slurred voice. Ree looked at him curiously as he pulled out another silver flask from the pocket of his overalls. Ree was confounded by Rivera's indiscrete question.

"How did you know?" she said.

"When I slew your dragon at the Waldorf, I noticed the doorman carried in a piece of luggage with a Nanking, China sticker on it." Rivera took a generous gulp from the flask. "I had friends who were traveling in Nanking during the Japanese invasion. I can guess what happened to you and your family. I am very sorry, my friend. Of course, one must not blame the common Japanese, but rather their sons of bitch masters, the industrialists of Japan and the industrialists the world over, who screw the little man. For the sake of the little man, my friend, you must allow me to show the world your paintings." Rivera once again caressed Ree and kissed her neck.

At first Ree resisted the dominating, obstinate man, but gradually she returned the affection. Rivera was only the second man Ree had ever kissed. Like so many women preceding her, Ree had become mesmerized by Rivera's stature as a well-known and influential artist. Though she found the oafish, blow-hearted man repulsive at first, she was now gaining a newfound respect for the man's commitment to his art and his desire for social change. Furthermore, the loneliness and strain from being uprooted twice had drawn her to someone she normally would not have been drawn to. Soon Ree and Rivera began a passionate yet tumultuous relationship.

In the beginning, Ree found it difficult to share a bed with Rivera. The only other men to lie with her did so as an act of violence and power. Sergeant Suzuki would not let go of her. But, bit by bit, she would cut away the portrait of Suzuki in her mind and replace it with a piece of Diego Rivera. Gradually, Ree began to enjoy her interludes with Rivera.

Their heated arguments were saved for after lovemaking when Rivera would request that he be allowed to showcase Ree's paintings. Each time Ree would refuse, saying, "Diego, I am a private person. My paintings are nobody's business but mine. Go to hell, Señor Rivera."

"Damn you," Señor Rivera would reply. "The yoke of the rich and powerful is heavy, and you will do nothing to help our beleaguered brothers and sisters," he scolded repetitively.

Ree could not admit to herself that this volatile relationship between two unyielding personalities would never last.

One morning, after a long night of painting and drinking, Ree groggily opened the front door to retrieve the daily newspaper she had recently subscribed to in order to keep up on the conflicts in Europe and her native China. As she bent over to lift the paper off the hallway floor, Ree glanced up to see the almost comical image of Frida Kahlo, sitting on the floor and holding a strong-smelling Turkish cigarette in one hand and a ripe mango in the other. Startled by Frida's presence, Ree jumped back.

Frida giggled. "Good morning, my pretty Chiquita. Invite me in. I will fix us both a needed cup of coffee and we can share this tasty mango." Frida walked into Ree's suite before Ree had a chance to offer permission.

"Miss Kahlo, it is nearly six in the morning! Why did you not knock?" Ree asked.

"I could not sleep, so I came to pay my respects to you. I didn't knock because I didn't wish to wake you had you been asleep. I assumed you would open your door eventually, for one reason or another," bantered Frida as she rummaged through Ree's kitchen for a coffee pot.

Though shocked by Frida's odd visit, Ree was in awe of the woman, having seen samples of her paintings in a gallery that Rivera had taken her to. Ree felt honored to be in the presence of such a great artist, but embarrassed at the same time, wondering whether Frida knew of her affair with Diego.

Once the coffee was prepared, the two women sat beside one another on the sofa.

"He doesn't love you," blurted Frida.

"What?" replied Ree, hardly able to believe her ears.

"My husband Diego does not love you. He enjoys the company of women. He would have intercourse with anything that has a hole between its legs. I suspect he would have an affair with the Statue of Liberty if he had a ladder."

Ree was puzzled. "You knew of our relationship, yet you did not object?"

"Diego and I have an open marriage. He may have his dalliances with whomever and I may have mine. Eventually, we always return to each other, perhaps because no one else can put up with us. I am very sorry, Ree. I know Diego can be very charming when he wants to be."

Ree shrugged her shoulders and smiled thinly. "I'm used to saying goodbye," she said philosophically.

Frida leaned closer to Ree. "Now that we have put my gordo husband to rest, what is this shit about you refusing a one-woman show? Your paintings have a voice that must be heard."

Ree clenched her fists in frustration. "I grow tired of having to answer to your husband, now I must answer to you: My paintings are my business and mine alone. You and your husband may change the world if you wish, but I simply want to be left alone."

"Ree, my friend, I know the goddamned *cabron* Japanese raped you. It is no surprise that you have so much anger. But if you share your hurt, the world will love you for it, and maybe it will prevent some future pretty Chinese girl from being raped," Frida said. She pressed her lips firmly against Ree's.

Ree felt no offense at Frida's advances. She had kissed Sylvia numerous times and found it pleasurable. She also wasn't surprised, having been informed by Diego of his wife's fondness for both sexes.

Ree began to laugh. "You and Diego are not like any gwai lahs I have ever met. I am not certain why I felt drawn to your husband. He is so fat and his eyes bulge out like a frog!"

"And what of me?" inquired Frida. "I have a unibrow, a moustache, and I am short with a twisted back."

Ree grinned and pressed her lips against Frida's. "At first I found both you and Mr. Rivera unpleasant to look at and a bit obnoxious."

Frida pulled her head back a few inches and caressed Ree's left cheek. "And what do you think of us now?"

"I still find you both unpleasant to look at and obnoxious. Who can say why one favors one over another?" Ree said.

Together the two women began to laugh hysterically. After the laughter died, Ree embraced Frida and whispered into her ear, "Diego is too fond of women. I know our time together will not last. I think like your husband, you want to love many women. I will be your girl until you tell me to leave. But I will never allow either of you to display my paintings to the world."

Rivera lost interest in Ree romantically once he learned his wife had gone to see her. Once again, Ree became involved in a love-hate relationship. As with Diego, she knew her liaison with Frida was not permanent. Nonetheless, she savored the time she had spent with Diego, and now she savored the time she was spending with Frida. She told Frida in a half-joking manner that she found the two of them unpleasant to look at, and obnoxious, and she meant every word of it. But, like so many men and women who had previously had affairs with the couple, Ree was drawn to them despite their physical shortcomings—perhaps attracted to their charm or zest for life, but not the fame that Ree never coveted.

Chapter 19

Ree's affair with Frida was now into its tenth week. To commemorate their anniversary, Ree purchased eight bright yellow roses and Chinese dim sum pastries she had purchased in New York's Chinatown. The Chinese considered eight a lucky number. Holding the roses, Ree entered her suite to await Frida's arrival with the giddy anticipation of a schoolgirl.

"For me?" came a glib voice from inside. "You are so kind."

Sylvia Farnsworth sat on the sofa, drawing heavily on a cigarette. With utter surprise, Ree let out a scream. The two had not seen or spoken to each other in weeks, even though Sylvia lived in the neighboring suite.

"How did you get in?" Ree asked.

"The maid allowed me in. It was not a problem, considering the fact that I'm paying the rent on your suite."

All of a sudden, Ree realized something was wrong. Something was missing.

"My paintings, they're gone!" Ree said excitedly.

"Oh, dear sister, you need not worry. They're being framed and hung in a very upscale gallery on Fifth Avenue," Sylvia explained.

"Bitch! Frida and Diego are responsible for this—and you, my very good friend, assisted them, no doubt," fumed Ree. "As I've said so many times: My paintings are for my eyes only! I will go to this gallery and cut the canvases to shreds!" In her fury, Ree hurled a vase at Sylvia.

Sylvia swiftly caught the expensive vase in midair. "Ree, my sister—and you are my sister after all we've been through—I have been paying your expenses as well as your mother's room and board back in England for some time now. Have you forgotten that you squandered your inheritance foolishly on liquor and games of luck? At first I paid your bills without complaint because you are the goddamned love of my life. But, if you want to waste your life, you will have to pay for it yourself."

Sylvia snatched the yellow roses from Ree's hands and placed them in water, then sat on the edge of the coffee table.

Ree hung her head in shame. "Yes, my life is a waste. You and Frida are the only ones who ever understood me and stood by me. Were it not for you and Frida and my painting, I would not have reason to live. Very well. Try to sell my paintings; and if by some miracle one should sell, I would like you to keep the money." She smiled at her friend. "Will you and Frida stand beside me at the opening so I won't feel totally naked?"

Sylvia gazed nervously at the ceiling. "Ree, I will never abandon you, but Frida has. I visited you to inform you of your art show, but at Frida's request I also came to tell you that she and Diego Rivera have returned to Mexico City."

Ree grabbed another vase and flung it at the wall, causing it to shatter loudly.

"Whore! She leaves me alone in a world of ugly, unfriendly lo fons. I knew Frida would leave someday, but I hoped it would be later, not sooner. She has a heart of stone to not say goodbye to me in person. Her bastard husband did not say goodbye to my face, either."

"Do not think too harshly of Frida or Diego," Sylvia said in defense of both. "Maybe she did not love you, but she was quite fond of you and respected you, as did Diego. They left to nursemaid some communist named Trotsky. The poor man would have been killed had he stayed in his motherland of Russia. And what is this silliness about lo fons being ugly and you being alone? I will not leave you. As I mentioned not sixty seconds ago, I will not abandon you, although there is not a lot to like about bitchy China women."

Ree gazed at her lifelong friend enigmatically. "It does appear you're all I have," she said.

Sylvia embraced Ree. They began to kiss each other passionately. That night the longtime friends slept together, covering themselves with the splendid silk sheets Sylvia's father had purchased while in China. The two women did not make love, but rather bantered about serious and non-serious things in life, as two close young women the world over often do while sipping expensive tequila, a drink that Frida and Diego had introduced to Ree, and which she had taken a deep liking to. Alone in the world, the two women became even closer than in their childhood days in China.

Finally, the momentous day arrived—Ree's opening night of her one-woman art show. Many of New York's wealthy and politically significant attended, having learned of the talented young Chinese artist from Rivera and Frida. Sylvia had arranged for the two of them to arrive at the gallery in a chauffeur-driven limousine. They donned costly gowns that Sylvia had custom tailored for the occasion, and for the first time in her life, Ree wore high-heeled shoes, much to her disdain.

As they entered the gallery, Ree and Sylvia were welcomed with a thunderous applause. Ree felt an odd blend of nervousness, apprehension, and euphoria. She was unaccustomed to having so many people staring at her, but all the while she felt a warm satisfaction that people actually approved of something she had created. It was an approval that she had never gotten from her parents.

Ree hobbled about on her formal dress shoes, cordially greeting everyone in the gallery. After several minutes, Ree could no longer stand teetering on spiked heels. In exasperation, she tore them off and tossed them to an attending waiter. "Burn those damn tools of torture! I refuse to be my grandmother," said Ree.

Sylvia stared at Ree with shock, but much to her surprise and relief, the guests once again applauded Ree, this time for her free-spirited, uninhibited nature.

"Burn these, too," Sylvia commanded, taking off her shoes as well and tossing them to the waiter.

Perhaps they are laughing at me behind my back, Ree worried to herself.

Laughing at her or not, Ree's paintings sold out that very night. The art critic from the *New York Times* praised Ree's work as "refreshing and enlightened." And, a few days following the gala opening, Ree received a telegram from Diego and Frida, congratulating her on the success of her first show.

Ree's success marked only the beginning of greater glory to come. Her popularity, as well as the prices of her paintings, continued to soar over the ensuing years. With World War II over, Ree and Sylvia moved to a penthouse apartment overlooking Central Park. Ree could now afford to have her mother relocated to an asylum on Long Island. Sylvia was now Ree's agent, confidante, and lover.

Ree had discovered a new peace and serenity in her life. There were rumors that Suzuki had died in 1943, but in a back niche of her soul she could still make out the lingering smug grin of Sergeant Suzuki. In early 1950 Ree and Sylvia returned to the bank of the chalk stream in England where they had left the portrait of Suzuki years earlier. Of course, the painting was nowhere in sight. In a futile attempt to find it, the women scoured every antique store, pub, and night lodging within a fifty-mile radius of the stream.

"Ree my love, it has been far more than a decade since we left the painting on the bank. That painting is gone forever. You are wealthy and famous now. Suzuki can no longer hurt you. No one can," Sylvia said.

"Suzuki lives. We did not destroy the painting, so Suzuki lives. I am sure of it."

"Sister, we have bigger fish to fry. We must return to New York to plan your new show at Rockefeller Center. Mr. Rockefeller is not accustomed to waiting for anyone."

Ree nodded her head in compliance.

The days blended into years. In 1970 Ree's mother passed on, after more than three decades of being institutionalized. Ree did not shed a single tear. There was no funeral, no memorial, nor words spoken. She had already shed enough tears years ago. To Ree, her mother had died in Nanking, decades ago. As with her father, she had mixed feelings of love and hate toward her, and to reflect on her would bring back the bitter memories of the Japanese invasion. Ree had her mother's body cremated, and like Sylvia's father, the ashes placed in an airtight urn. Someday Ree would place her mother beside Father Chou in the Nanking Cemetery, once mainland China became open to visitors.

As Ree's prestige spread, she received an invitation to show her work from an old and familiar name. The official letter was from the Generalissimo himself, Chiang Kai-shek, who was now the supreme leader of Taiwan, having fled the mainland when the communists took control of China in the late forties. Ree tore the invitation to shreds. Despite the decades that had passed, Ree still harbored feelings of betrayal toward Chiang, remembering how he refused to assist her family during the Japanese invasion. Ree shared a bottle of her favorite brand of tequila with Sylvia the day the Generalissimo died in 1975.

By the mid-seventies Ree was at the height of her fame and popularity. Her paintings fetched sums as high as half a million dollars. Now in her middle years, Ree began to drink heavily again. The ghost of a Japanese sergeant again would not allow her peace of mind. Then, in 1977 a call came to Ree's penthouse and again her world was turned upside down.

Chapter 20

As Ree had done for decades, she painted throughout much of the night, sometimes past daybreak. Then she would sleep well into the afternoon. It was nearly two in the afternoon when the phone rang. Sylvia, who usually rose several hours before Ree, answered the phone.

"Who the hell is calling me at this hour?" cried Ree.

"It is the ambassador from mainland China calling. He says it is of the utmost importance that he talk to you," said Sylvia, handing Ree the phone.

With her head still buried in the pillow, Ree rested the phone against her ear. She half-heartedly greeted the caller. After hearing the caller's request, she said, "No. And if there is any part of 'no' that you do not understand, ask your mother," quipped Ree after hearing the invitation for a one-woman show in Nanking.

"Sister, have you lost your bloody mind? It would be a great honor to receive an invitation by the Chinese government to display your paintings in Nanking. And have you forgotten your promise to your mother? To someday bury her with your father? In three years we'll both be sixty. Who can say how much more time you'll have to go home again?"

Ree buried her head in her pillow. Rolling over, she flung the pillow at Sylvia. "Sister, China is no longer my home. They just want to put me on display like a monkey at a circus sideshow. I'm already dancing with a leash around my neck for the gwai lahs on the Gold Mountain. I never liked New York, living in this box six hundred feet above the pavement. I miss the feeling of my bare feet on the warm spring earth, watching my winter melons grow. You are a gwai lah, Sylvia. You do not know what it feels like to have yellow skin. Before I became famous, they would not serve me in the hotel restaurant."

"Damn you, Ree. You never told me you hated living in eye fowl or that they would not serve you in the restaurant. Now, let me enlighten you, my yellow lover. When we were children in China, I went to the school for diplomats' children. One day I professed to my classmates that I was in love with the most beautiful Chinese girl in the world. They teased me and beat on me in the playground, calling me an egg—white on the outside and yellow on the inside. My best friend and lover of four decades, you have no idea what pain and sacrifices I have made for you. In my youth, I wanted to be a fashion designer, but I gave up my dreams to nurture yours." Tears flowed down Sylvia's face.

Ree rose off the bed, her nude body embracing Sylvia. "I'm so sorry. We both have a lot to learn about each other, even after all these years. I owe you so much—my career, my health, my life."

Holding each other, the two women gazed at their images in a full-length mirror. Ree touched her hair, fondling the white streaks that ran through her once jet-black hair.

"Ree, you're still that beautiful Chinese girl I fell in love with when I was six. Your body is still lean and firm," said Sylvia.

"And you are still the beautiful gwai lah girl I met when I was six. Your hair still resembles spun gold."

"My gold hair comes out of a bottle," Sylvia responded.

The two women began to giggle as they did when they were children. When the laughter died down, Sylvia took on a serious gaze.

"Go home, Ree. I think it will give you peace of

mind."

Ree stroked Sylvia's long blond hair. "Sister, my soul was stolen. The Japanese invaders took my precious winter melons, they butchered..."

"And so on and so on. You do not have to remind me of what happened to you in Nanking. I was there, remember? You need to bury something other than your mother in Nanking. You were born in China, you have Chinese blood flowing in your veins. Try to remember the good moments while you bury the bad ones," Sylvia advised.

Ree stood observing her naked body in the mirror. She thought of all the pain and loss in her life. But now that she was in her middle years, she had found a small scrap of peace. Her paintings sold for outrageous prices, and she was sharing her life with a woman she loved very much. Perhaps Sylvia was right. Perhaps she should return to China, if for no other reason than to honor her countrymen and women who did not survive the rape of Nanking.

"Yes, Sylvia, I am Chinese. I'm going home."

"My lover, I am also Chinese. We'll go together," Sylvia said, and kissed Ree.

Ree called the Chinese ambassador to apologize for her rude manner, and accepted the invitation. She would create a painting to memorialize the victims who perished during the Chinese holocaust.

With a passion Ree had not felt in years, she immediately set to work on her Nanking painting. The seven-foot by thirteen-foot canvas dominated the length of one entire wall in Ree's suite. The monumental painting was to be a homage to Goya's masterpiece, *The Execution of the Third Day of May*. Like Goya's painting, Ree's painting was to be a powerful statement of senseless genocide. In place of Napoleon's troops executing innocent Spanish citizens, Ree would depict

Japanese soldiers executing innocent Chinese citizens.

Given only six weeks' notice, Ree painted feverishly, day and night, sleeping very little and living on coffee, tequila, and sandwiches so that she could paint and eat at the same time. Sylvia stood by Ree, preparing the sandwiches and coffee, and massaging her shoulders when she grew fatigued.

Ree finished the painting only four days before their departure for Nanking. As they stared at it, Ree and Sylvia breathed a sigh of relief. Ree had to tear away part of the door frame in order to remove the enormous painting from her suite. Her painting was evocative and was praised by art critics and laymen alike.

After a whirlwind of press conferences and interviews, Ree and Sylvia finally boarded a plane, along with Mother Zu's ashes and the Nanking painting, headed for Ree's homeland China.

"We're going home, Mother," Ree whispered under her breath to the funeral urn. Like Sylvia, who had brought her father's ashes to New York decades before, Ree had purchased a separate seat for the urn that held her mother's ashes.

After what seemed like an endless flight with endless stopovers, the two women arrived in China and boarded a special VIP train in Beijing. They were the only passengers except for the political and security escorts who accompanied them. As Ree watched the passing scenery of her native country, she became physically ill, much to the concern of Sylvia and her escorts. Fearing the worst, the women's primary chaperone ordered the train to be stopped while a physician was flown from Beijing to the train. Ree's condition turned out to be nothing more than butterflies and anxiety. She assured the Chinese escort and Sylvia that she was fine. It was just a simple case of fatigue.

But Ree's illness went beyond that. There was a feeling of no longer belonging. After a forty-year absence, she could scarcely speak or understand Chinese any longer, and the dignitaries who welcomed her in Beijing behaved as though she was a yellow lo fon rather than a fellow countryman.

When the train approached Nanking, Sylvia burst into their private train compartment where Ree napped.

"Ree! Wake up. Nanking is dead ahead. Come look!"

Less than a mile in the distance was Nanking and the familiar ancient wall that surrounded the city.

It looks so much smaller than what I remember, Ree thought as she looked upon the wall after so many years.

The train screeched to a halt at the station, which was close to the city wall. From there, the two women and their chaperone boarded a sleek, black Cadillac limousine. The primary tunnel through the wall was now widened to accommodate modern traffic. Many of the old buildings Ree remembered from her childhood remained. Absent were the ox and horse-drawn carts. The motor traffic was heavier and the pedestrian traffic as thick as ever. The motorcade sped past the Sun Yat-sen memorial, and Ree reflected on how most of Nanking had not changed since she saw it last.

Ree wrestled with her demons. She clenched her eyes tightly as the limousine threaded through the tunnel wall. No more than a few yards from the tunnel marked the very spot where Father Chou had fallen to his death. Equally close was the place atop the wall where she and Song began to be intimate, only to be interrupted by the beginning of the Japanese artillery bombardment.

Ree blocked out the horrible memories as best she could, thinking of the more joyous times when she played atop the city wall with her kid sister, Mi.

"Ladies, here we are. I am sure the two of you would like to relax and freshen up after the long journey," said their elderly chaperone. "The Royal Jade Hotel has been recently renovated and is the finest hotel in Nanking."

Ree began to scream hysterically, crouching in terror

on the floor of the limousine.

"Idiot!" Sylvia shouted. "Bloody idiots! The Royal Jade Hotel is the very establishment where my girlfriend was raped and tortured! You bloody bureaucrats should have done your homework."

Shocked, the chaperone's mouth dropped. In a halted voice she said, "I am so sorry, Miss Gong, Miss Farnsworth. It was indeed very callous of us not to have planned your accommodations more carefully." She turned to the chauffeur. "Take us to the Hilton. Immediately!"

Arriving at the newly built Nanking Hilton, Sylvia and a security guard assisted a badly shaken Ree into the finest suite in the hotel. The room was adorned throughout with freshly cut flowers, and a basket of fresh fruit sat on the coffee table.

Sylvia put Ree onto the bed and placed a damp cloth on Ree's forehead. Then Sylvia crawled into bed beside the woman she had loved so much of her life, whispering about the more pleasant times they had spent together in Kiangsu Province and Nanking.

Chapter 21

Ree's visions of being strapped to a bed and repeatedly raped by Sergeant Suzuki began to fade. Having regained her composure, Ree and Sylvia went to a luncheon the following day. The luncheon was meant as a casual introduction to the prominent political figures who would be present at the forthcoming ceremony honoring the victims of the Nanking massacre.

With great fanfare, Ree and Sylvia entered the very same civic center in which Chiang Kai-shek held tenuous direction over the government affairs of China before the Japanese conquest of Nanking. Countless camera flashbulbs blinded the two women while Ree received grand applause. Such adulation did not impress or frighten Ree, having been a public figure for numerous years. In fact, she had become quite complacent toward the attention.

A smiling, middle-aged Chinese man dressed in a finely tailored suit firmly shook the hands of Ree and Sylvia. "Miss Gong, Miss Farnsworth, we are all deeply honored to meet in person China's greatest living woman artist and her secretary. I am Wu Chee, the mayor of Nanking."

"I, too, am honored to return to my homeland after such a long absence," remarked Ree, fighting the urge to laugh aloud over the estimation that she was China's greatest female artist and that they had the impression that Sylvia was her secretary, when in fact she was her lover and a titled English noble.

"Dear ladies, please further allow me to introduce

you to one of Nanking's most distinguished citizens, Mr. Hong Bao. He is the man most responsible for the memorial, and most of the cost has been paid for with Mr. Hong's own personal funds."

"Mr. Hong, it is also a pleasure to…" Ree stopped in mid-sentence as her eyes turned to address the civic-minded leader.

Both she and Sylvia were taken aback to see a terribly disfigured man standing before them.

Ree struggled for words. "I…I…"

"Miss Gong, you need not apologize for a lack of words," Mr. Hong said. "Few people react differently when they first lay eyes on me. My features are a souvenir from the Japanese soldiers. They laughed when they doused my face with gasoline and set it afire because I refused to rape a nun. But such is life. I have no regrets over my decision to disobey those bastards."

"You poor man," said Ree. "We all suffered so much at the hands of those sons of bitches."

Ree felt a sharp poke to her ribs from Sylvia, her way of warning her girlfriend to watch her language.

The mayor attempted to lighten the mood. "Mr. Hong also raised funds for the construction of Nanking's new children's hospital."

"Mr. Hong, you are kind and generous. I was born and raised in Kiangsu Province, but I do not recall a Hong Bao when I was growing up there. Has your family lived in this region long?" Ree inquired.

"Most certainly. You would not remember my family because they were only lowly peasants, and not likely to mingle with the wealthy Gong family. It is not likely that such a lovely woman with an angel face like yours would ever speak with someone like me, even when I possessed a normal face," Mr. Hong said.

Angel face. The words cut into Ree's soul. Feeling faint, her body began to sway.

Sylvia quickly grabbed her friend to keep her from

falling. "What's wrong?"

Ree smiled politely as Sylvia wiped her perspiring face with a handkerchief. "Excuse me, gentlemen. I am just tired, what with all this excitement. I will see all of you at the ceremony on Saturday. I promise I will be well by then."

Ree sprinted away with Sylvia in tow, leaving everyone worried about their native daughter's welfare.

"Ree, I suspect there is something more going on here than just fatigue and this emotional baggage that you have carried with you to Nanking. What else is there, my love?"

Ree looked out the car window at the passing buildings with a contemplative gaze. "Sylvia, please, not now. Give me a moment to catch my breath."

When they entered their suite, Ree immediately uncorked a bottle of brandy that was sitting on the coffee table. She gulped it greedily, then slipped off her shoes and threw herself onto the bed. "Sylvia, lie with me please."

Honoring Ree's request, Sylvia removed her shoes and climbed onto the bed.

"It's *him*," blurted Ree.

"It's who?"

"It's the monster, Sergeant Suzuki Toro, the monster in my dreams for forty years. He was at the luncheon."

Sylvia stared with shock at Ree. "You can't be serious. How can that be? Which one of those respected Chinese citizens could be a former Japanese soldier?"

Ree sat up, taking another gulp of brandy. "The civic-minded Hong Bao," she stammered.

Sylvia laughed. "How bloody ridiculous. Mr. Hong is highly regarded by his peers. It appears he is a lifelong resident of Nanking. His face was badly disfigured by the Japanese soldiers. He would have as much reason to hate the Japanese as we do."

Ree shook her head. "I know what I'm saying. China

in 1937 was a goddamned chaotic mess. Many records were destroyed or lost. A man as clever as Suzuki could have easily taken over the identity of someone with no surviving family—someone perhaps Suzuki slaughtered himself. And what better way to hide his true identity than to disfigure his face with gasoline?"

"But you have not explained how you can be so sure it is Suzuki," Sylvia said.

"Angel face. Suzuki had the audacity to refer to me as 'angel face' when he was violating me. Mr. Hong called me angel face. Plus, two more clues hit me like a train head-on that I was looking into the eyes of the devil. Part of Hong's bottom left ear is missing, even though the flames that burned his face did not touch his ears. It is a clean cut, caused by my teeth when I bit it off when he first assaulted me. Secondly, I recognize that raspy voice, not unlike the sound of fingernails on a chalkboard, and he has the blocky body of Suzuki."

"That is a tad thin, my love," Sylvia said. "Many gentlemen have raspy voices. His ear could have been sliced off in some other way, and 'angel face' is a rather common nickname. He seemed friendly enough. Why didn't he recognize you?"

"The monster has raped hundreds and killed thousands. Why would he remember my face from so many? Or, maybe he's just a good actor."

"My sister, I've also met your monster. Father and I rescued you from him, remember? I do not see in Hong what you see as the Japanese war criminal."

"That heartless beast has lived inside me every day and every night for forty years. If a thousand winters had passed and he had burned his face into a blackened lump of coal I would somehow feel his presence." Ree gave a subdued chuckle. "It is funny. I can see forever in my mind the face of Suzuki, but it is sometimes difficult to picture Song's face."

"Yes, I remember you once said that some years ago.

I also have difficulty seeing the faces of past loves." A melancholy look came over Sylvia's face. "Forgetting Mr. Suzuki for a moment, answer me a question, please. If given the choice, would you want your Lieutenant Song lying with you now, or me here beside you?"

"That is an unfair question. I believe I loved Song more than any man I've ever loved. I was only a teenager. It was a different time and a different world." Ree threw her lifelong companion a grin. "We've loved and hated each other for half a century, and you are the only one I would care to spend the rest of my days with. I love you, Lady Farnsworth," said Ree, running her fingers through Sylvia's hair.

Sylvia sat up and sat on the edge of the bed with Ree. "It is good that you feel so strongly for me. We are both not easy people to live with. Song would have strangled you long ago had he lived. As for your Mr. Hong a.k.a. Suzuki, assuming he is who you say he is, what do you propose to do about it?"

Ree kissed Sylvia's ear. "Isn't it obvious? I want the monster dead. He took everything from me. His life would be a very small form of repayment."

"You're talking about murder? Last time I checked it is illegal, not only in China, but everywhere else, too. Why not let the authorities handle the matter?"

"No way. It would be his word against mine. It would be difficult to prove. Forty years have passed since the Rape of Nanking. Only a handful have ever been tried and convicted. The son of a bitch Sergeant Suzuki once told me he was a god. Now it is my turn to play God."

"And how do you propose to go about committing the first original sin?"

"I want to see the monster die while I'm watching!" Ree screamed. "Just as he watched my father kill himself and as he watched my grandmother die and as he watched my sister bleed to death after he raped her! At the grand memorial ceremony and dinner planned for this Saturday, I will lay a trap for him. On that day they will undrape my masterpiece. I insisted that they serve my favorite winter melon soup as the first course." Ree smiled like a mischievous child. "As routine, the waitresses will push a cart carrying a tureen of winter melon soup along with several individual bowls, one for each guest. One of the waitresses will begin to fill each bowl with soup. At that moment I will leap up suddenly, pretending to see an old friend from the past, accidentally spilling the bowl meant for Mr. Hong. With endless apologies, I will take a fresh empty bowl and offer to serve Mr. Hong personally. At that point, I will slip poison into the bastard's soup just before I place it in front of him."

Sylvia shook her head. "Your window of opportunity is quite narrow. You will never pull it off."

"I can, and I will have the pleasure of watching Suzuki die slowly and with great pain. But whatever pain he feels, it will never be payment in full."

"There is one glitch that comes to mind. Ree, dear love, you are too modest. If you were to purchase poison in a very public place the whole world would know that the world's greatest Chinese female artist had bought it. Allow me to do this one part of the plan for you. I will pretend to be a visiting professor, teaching at Nanking University," offered Sylvia. "I'll explain that I have rats in my apartment."

Ree began to cackle with delight. "Sylvia, my life partner, I could not live without you. We can both have the pleasure of watching my demon being put to rest," she said, giving Sylvia a hug.

Abruptly Sylvia pushed Ree away. "I will only buy the poison for you. Nothing more. I will not sit with you and watch even a monster like Suzuki die."

"Sylvia, I only want the bad dreams to go away. Suzuki has a price he must pay, and I have waited for forty years for payment."

"You ask too much. The monster cannot return anything that he has taken from you. Ree, dear girl, you were always so impetuous. You were always the one willing to jump naked into the cold swift waters of the Yangtze, while I would only dangle my bare feet in the water. I was always the follower, never the leader. But this time the follower is telling the leader to not go forward. I can promise you that you will not sleep better at night if you kill the monster in your dreams. But if you must insist on this obscene act, I will purchase the poison, then return to New York. You can make some excuse as to why I left early."

"Sylvia, my beloved, you do what you feel is best for you. I do this for me, not for you. I could pretend it is all for my family and my Lieutenant Song that Suzuki slaughtered, or even for the hundreds of thousands that Suzuki and his soldiers killed, but it would be a lie. I do it for my own peace of mind. If I am caught, I will take full responsibility. I will not allow anyone to hurt you. I do thank you for helping me." She planted a kiss on Sylvia's cheek.

In response, Sylvia turned her head away, rose off the bed, and left their suite, speaking nothing else. The door she slammed behind her expressed more than words.

The following day a small packet of white powder sat on Ree's nightstand. Sylvia was nowhere to be found. Under the packet of powder was a note from Sylvia, stating it contained strychnine, a very potent poison, and that it should easily serve its purpose. In closing, Ree's lover, confidante, associate and best friend wrote in bold letters: *You commit this sin, the beast will be raping you a second time. Goodbye. With love, Sylvia.*

Indignant, Ree read Sylvia's note several times. She felt a profound sense of abandonment by her lifelong companion.

My lover could not even say goodbye to me in person, Ree thought, and reached for her bottle of tequila. She began to drink herself into a stupor, pondering whether Sylvia's goodbye note meant goodbye for now, or goodbye forever.

Chapter 22

The days passed with an agonizing slowness, although Ree had few idle moments, attending an endless procession of luncheons, press conferences and photo shoots, all of which she found tedious and repetitive. All the while Ree remained preoccupied with her obsession to kill the man responsible for so much sorrow in her life, as well as in the lives of countless others.

Eventually, the day Ree had anxiously awaited arrived. Ree stood on her balcony sipping tequila and watching the brilliant orange sunrise. For most of the night she had been pacing in her room, drinking the brandy she was so fond of, then switching to the tequila introduced to her by Rivera and Frida. With one last swallow of tequila remaining in the bottle, Ree saluted the rising sun. She then hurled the empty bottle at the sun as a way of insulting God.

"Where is this God Sylvia told me of? Where were you when I was being raped and my family was being murdered?" she screamed at the top of her lungs. She stretched her body over the railing, her hand extended in a ludicrous attempt to touch the sun. She then reentered the suite, dressed, and called down to the front desk to request a driver and a limousine. Several hours still remained until the memorial ceremony, but Ree still had one more obligation to complete.

The long black Cadillac glided along the meandering road toward the Nanking cemetery. As with most cemeteries, the grounds were tranquil, abundant with lovely shade trees and well-manicured lawns. The limousine stopped beside the Gong family plot. Three groundskeepers were already busily digging up the gravesite of the patriarch, Gong Chou.

"Miss Gong, we're nearly finished," said one of the men.

Ree carefully placed the urn containing her mother's ashes beside her father's grave. "Please place my mother in my father's coffin when you are ready, and please do so with great care," she ordered.

The men nodded in compliance. Once the task was done, the men refilled the hole. When the second chore was completed, Ree handed each of the three men a substantial tip. She then ordered them to leave so that she could be alone with her family.

It was so long ago, Ree thought, the last time she laid eyes on her family and Song, who she had buried in the Gong plot years before. Ree laughed half-heartedly. "One last farewell to my family. I do not know what to say, for we were never very close. Today I will kill the man who took all of you away from me. Maybe we did love each other, but we did not know how to show it. But all of the things we could not say to each other we will say some other day when we're together again.

"Father, you took your own life rather than violate me. I realize now you did it for me, not just to save your pride. Song, my beautiful man, do not judge me for loving Sylvia, as well. You were my first love and Sylvia my second."

Ree kissed the gravestones of her family and Song, then returned to the car.

In the remaining hours before the memorial and dinner party, Ree had the driver take her the short distance to the high bluff overlooking the wide and long Yangtze River. Pictures of her previous life in China flashed before her—the ripening winter melons, her first kisses with Sylvia and Song, interplay between the countless horrors inflicted on her and her family by Suzuki...all the while hearing Sylvia's warning that she would find no peace by killing Suzuki. She watched commercial and pleasure boats power their way up and down the river until it was time to leave for the ceremony.

Ree rehearsed in her mind over and over every move she would make and every word she would say in order to carry out her plot. She was so engrossed with the choreography of her murder plan that she didn't notice the limousine had arrived at the civic center where the event was to take place.

"Miss Gong...Miss Gong?" said the driver. "We have arrived."

Ree snapped out of her absorbed thoughts to once again hear the loud cheers of Nanking's citizenry welcoming their native daughter. An Honor Guard opened the limousine door. Ree was greeted by Nanking's mayor and the city's most prominent businessman, Hong Bao—the man Ree was certain was the war criminal Sergeant Suzuki Toro. Together they escorted Ree into an immense hall, specifically designed for such lavish events.

Walking the gauntlet of applauding well-wishers and media cameramen flashing their bulbs at her, Ree returned a forced smile as the mayor held her right arm and Hong her left. The Nanking High School marching band played the lo fon tune "God Bless America." Ree could not bear to look at Hong. She fixed her eyes on the adoring crowd.

Ree was escorted to a table fronting the stage, where her painting hung draped with a white sheet. After being seated, the governor of Kiangsu took center stage and began a colorful oratory of not only China's, but the world's responsibility to never allow a tragedy like the Rape of Nanking to happen again.

"Miss Gong, you have suffered a great deal from the

Japanese who invaded your country. I offer my sincerest sympathy to you," said Hong Bao.

Ree immediately recognized the slip of his tongue. He said *your* country, not *our* country. Ree took his remark as a patronizing insult, although it was intended as an effort by Hong to make small talk. She fought the urge to strike Hong on the spot. Instead, she said with a strained grin, "Mr. Hong, my sympathies to you, also. It appears the bastard Japs abused you as much as they did me."

Hong, as well as the others sitting at Ree's table, appeared speechless and uncomfortable with Ree's language and racist term.

Hong nodded. "I apologize, Miss Gong, if I dug up some unpleasant memories for you. Yes, I have also suffered. I had my own dragons to slay," said Hong. "I concur that the Japanese committed serious and immoral crimes in Nanking. In truth, many Japanese to this day deny the Rape of Nanking even occurred."

Ree's left leg began to shake uncontrollably, and she could barely contain her emotions as she sat next to the man she had despised and feared for so long. "Do you hate the Japanese as much as I do?" Ree said, trying again to get a rise out of Hong.

Hong gazed directly into Ree's eyes. It was difficult to discern any emotion on the man's face due to his disfigurement.

"I pity the Japanese soldier of that era more than hate him. Honor and duty was and is very important to the Japanese culture. It is doubtful that any soldiers participating in the Rape of Nanking felt any joy or pride from what they did," Hong said with a wavering voice.

"May they be cursed forever in hell," cried Ree, angry that she didn't strike a harsher chord with Hong.

The other guests were embarrassed once more by the guest of honor's brashness, and once more they were at a loss for words. Thankfully for them, the governor, who had just ended his speech, began to slowly undrape Ree's enormous painting, which was destined to hang in a new building honoring those who perished in the Chinese holocaust.

As Ree intended, the painting was a homage to Goya's masterpiece depicting Napoleonic era soldiers executing innocent Spanish civilians. Ree's highly provocative and emotional painting depicted naked Chinese men, women, and children being executed by Japanese soldiers. In strong contrast, Ree painted the massive painting in black, white, and grays, with one exception of a Japanese soldier bearing the rank of sergeant painted in bright colors. The Suzuki look-alike smiled comically as he observed the horrid massacre.

Several, including the governor and mayor, requested that Ree take the stage to give a brief speech for this special occasion. Ree gulped down a full glass of wine. Nervously, she ascended the stage. The crowd erupted into a standing ovation of thunderous applause.

Standing before the microphone, Ree mustered the courage to look Hong directly in the eyes. She began to visualize in place of the middle-aged, disfigured Chinese businessman the young, unscarred Japanese soldier who had brutalized her and her family some four decades ago.

"My fellow countrymen and women, we are here today to honor the estimated three-hundred thousand innocent Chinese butchered by the Japanese military invaders in 1937. More victims than those killed by the atomic bombings of Hiroshima and Nagasaki combined. If I have learned anything from this tragedy, it is that there are no evil nations or nationalities, only evil people. Like some of you present today, I have lost much." Her voice began to waver. She fixed her eyes upon Hong. "One Japanese soldier stole everything from me; everything except my soul. So, I say to all of you, there will be a reckoning someday. Be strong, my brothers and sisters of China, and take comfort that these murderers will have their reckoning."

Returning to her seat, Ree received yet another standing ovation. She saw large droplets of tears rolling down Hong's face.

"Miss Gong, I congratulate you on your profound painting and profound speech. The painting speaks far more than the volumes of cold statistics can." He touched his hand atop Ree's.

Pretending not to notice, Ree pulled her hand away and took a sip of water.

"Miss Gong, please allow me to mention that Mr. Hong has personally paid your fee of one-hundred thousand dollars so that your excellent painting will hang in our new memorial building for all time," stated the mayor, who sat across from Ree.

Ree nodded in pretentious politeness.

The dinner's first course was winter melon soup, which Ree had requested. Two young women rolled a cart up to their table. The rich, pleasant aroma from the soup brought smiles to everyone. One woman poured the savory broth and chunks of melon into individual bowls. Then the other woman placed a bowl in front of each guest.

Ree, being the guest of honor, was served first, then the others around the circular table. Hong would be the last one served. Ree began to perspire slightly. Her breathing became labored. Images of Suzuki violating her flashed through her mind. Two sides of her conscience fought for dominance. One side whispered that her plan to murder Hong was justified; she had the right. The more benevolent side whispered that retribution did not belong to her; someday he would pay, but not by her hand.

Time finally ran out. The server began to pour the soup meant for Hong. Leaping off her chair, Ree cried out, "Mr. Chin!" while purposely knocking the bowl of soup from the young woman's hands. Ree's darker side had won.

Behaving in an overly apologetic fashion, Ree quickly lifted a clean bowl from the cart, all the while insisting that she serve the bowl to Mr. Hong herself. During the confusion, Ree snatched the packet of poison that was strapped to her thigh with an elastic band. Though highly stressed, Ree acted beautifully as the embarrassed klutz. Without detection, she placed the powder into the bowl, then dutifully placed the simmering soup on the table before Hong.

Hong, as well as everyone else at the table, reassured Ree that her accident was of no consequence and that she should not be embarrassed by it. And, with the accident out of the way, everyone began to dine on the delicious winter melon soup. Ree began to eat, keeping a watchful eye on Hong. She had not eaten winter melon soup in a long time, and though she found it not as good as how Mother Zu and Mama On used to prepare it, it brought back pleasant memories of her youth. But such happy recollections were only fleeting. She knew she had to stay focused on the task at hand.

As Hong consumed the soup, Ree waited anxiously for him to react to the poison.

"Do you fear death, Mr. Hong?" she inquired curiously.

A subtle smile registered on Hong's distorted face. "Of course not. I am a disfigured man who has been alone most of his life. I will die alone, even though I may be surrounded by people. We all die alone, do we not? Tell me, Miss Gong, do you think it's possible for a man to change? Can a man conquer his evil side and become a good man?"

Ree looked into Hong's eyes, searching for his true self. "Damn your soul, Suzuki. I wish I knew. Only Sylvia's gwai lah god can answer that." Again the two sides of Ree's conscience dueled. Anger and hatred fought pity and guilt. "Stop! Do not eat anymore soup!" Ree shouted, firmly gripping Hong's hand, which held his spoon.

Hong looked at Ree with an enigmatic smile through his thick scars. His mouth began to foam. Then, with a hard crash, he fell to the floor, writhing with wild convulsions.

"Please! Someone call an ambulance, Mr. Hong is seriously ill!" screamed Ree, holding Hong in an attempt to subdue his shaking.

Pandemonium prevailed among the hundreds in attendance. Soon a thick circle of concerned and curious guests surrounded the fallen man.

Within a few minutes, Hong stopped breathing. Frantically, Ree searched with her fingers for obstructions in his mouth. She removed a few bits of melon, then pressed her mouth to Hong's, blowing air into the man's lungs. Despite her valiant efforts, Hong could not be saved and was pronounced dead en route to the hospital.

As expected, everyone presumed Hong had died from heart failure or suffocated from a piece of wayward food that had lodged in his windpipe. But Ree knew that Hong hadn't died from either. She sat in her darkened suite, drinking both brandy and tequila late into the night, thinking about what she had done.

I took the life of the monster in my nightmares, yet I feel no joy or relief from it. Why? Ree thought.

Sylvia was correct. Ree did not sleep any better. She walked out onto the balcony to gaze at the city wall in the distance.

"I had the right to kill Suzuki, didn't I? Sylvia, my lover and friend, if only you were here to tell me what I should do," Ree mouthed under her breath.

Chapter 23

Ree had booked the earliest flight available to return to her home in New York City before an autopsy could be performed on Hong's body. The following morning she was chauffeured to the train station, bound for Beijing, then to New York. She had given notice to no one that she was leaving. Repeatedly she rationalized her killing of Hong Bao.

As they arrived at the train station, the chauffeur opened the car door for Ree. But Ree did not step out. Instead, she sat staring into space. The dutiful chauffeur continued to hold the door, puzzled as to why his passenger wasn't getting out, but did not dare question the famous artist.

"Take me to the primary police station," Ree finally ordered.

At the police station, Ree walked inside with a trembling gate, and in a halted voice, confessed her crime. Stunned by Ree's unbelievable statement, the police summoned a high-ranking official from Beijing. Given Ree's status, she was not placed in a prison cell, but was returned to her hotel suite to await the arrival of a government official.

A polite knock reported from the front door of the suite. Ree promptly opened it to find a well-dressed man with thinning gray hair, a round face, and a cordial smile that expressed a fatherly warmth.

"Miss Gong," he said, "I am deeply honored to be in the presence of one of the world's great artists. I am Wu Sin, special aide to China's honorable Chairman. Now, what is this nonsense that you are a murderer?"

They sat on the sofa. Ree introduced the official to her favorite drink, tequila. The man was quite taken with the Mexican drink.

Calmly and without tears, Ree told Wu Sin the long and very involved story of her life, and of her reasons and methods in taking the life of Sergeant Suzuki, who was posing as the Chinese businessman Hong Bao. Once she finished her story, the official placed a comforting hand on Ree's shoulder.

"Miss Gong, you are a good and honorable woman. My family also suffered at the hands of those evil men. I was only a boy of ten when the Japanese soldiers raped my mother and sister. I watched my father beg for mercy as they did their foul deeds. My poor father was then decapitated. Then they butchered my mother and sister. In a fortunate twist of fate, they also shot me and left me for dead, but, unlike the rest of my family, I managed to survive my wounds." Wu Sin began to sob uncontrollably.

In an unusual reversal of roles, it was Ree who began to comfort the government official, who was nearing hysterics. Ree embraced the man firmly, as a loving mother would her infant. "Mr. Wu, we both have wounded souls that will never heal," she said, and poured him another glass of tequila. She then wiped away his tears.

Wu gulped down the strong liquor, coughing a bit as he swallowed. "Miss Gong, you are a kind woman. You had every good reason to kill that devil in a man's body. I will inform the authorities to list Hong's death as a case of heart failure. Aside from your fame as a truly excellent artist, you will be hailed as a hero for attempting to save the man's life. Miss Gong, the truth will never leave this room. I think the gwai lahs have a saying: 'We'll sweep it under the door.'"

"That's rug. Sweep it under the rug," corrected Ree.

She grinned with subtle amusement at the man's offer. "Mr. Sin, I do so very much appreciate your gift of a lie to protect me from punishment by the Chinese legal system. But I cannot accept, even though you're doing so to shelter me from further pain, embarrassment, and scandal. I humbly decline your sincere proposal."

The official could hardly believe Ree's words. "Miss Gong, you fail to understand what I have explained to you. I am offering you an out. You can return to the Gold Mountain and live in double happiness with your gentleman friend, if you have one. The world will never know of your crime—which was no crime in my estimation. Men like Hong or Suzuki need killing."

"I would always know I took a life," Ree said. "For four decades I could think of nothing but killing that bastard. But as my lover pointed out, I would sleep no better if I carried out the act. As usual, Sylvia was right."

Wu Sin gazed at Ree with some confusion. "Isn't Sylvia a lo fon female's first name?"

"Why, yes, it is," Ree replied in a matter-of-fact manner.

The official rolled his eyes in disgust once he realized the woman and artist he admired so greatly had a same-sex lover. "Miss Gong, since you have refused to accept my generous offer, I have no alternative but to have the authorities place you under arrest."

The Nanking authorities arrived at the hotel and took Ree into custody. Under heavy guard she was taken to the Beijing high security prison. Ree signed a full confession to being the sole individual responsible for the murder of Hong Bao. And because the wheels of the Chinese legal system spin faster than the American legal system, the trial lasted but a few days and Ree was immediately sentenced to death by firing squad. And, to add further insult, Ree's estate would be billed for the bullets used in her execution.

Once the news of Ree's confession and death sentence

became public knowledge, swarms of sympathizers rallied in protest at the prison gates. Ree, awaiting her execution, would sit each day in the corner of her bare prison cell, drawing countless pictures of faces she remembered from the past and present. She refused all requests for interviews by the news media, as well as refusing any legal representation or assistance from the American government.

On her fifth day of incarceration, a prison guard came to Ree's cell. As usual, she sat with folded legs on the floor, drawing portraits and morose scenes of the Chinese holocaust. From outside she could hear the shouts from the throngs of protestors, keeping vigil just outside the prison gates. "Miss Gong," said the guard. "You have a visitor. Please come with me."

"I distinctly said that I do not wish to see anyone," Ree said. "Whoever it may be can screw themselves."

The guard ignored her hostility and politely insisted again that she accompany him to the visiting room.

"Very well. At least I will briefly escape that incessant shouting from the protestors," said Ree, walking barefoot down the corridor.

The prison guard opened the door to the room. There, to her astonishment, Ree saw Sylvia sitting at a table, puffing heavily on a cigarette.

"Damn you, Sylvia, you should not have come," said Ree.

"Darling, I would have come sooner, but being tequila drunk for three days after I left you, I didn't bother to read the papers or watch the telly."

Sylvia rose off her chair and embraced Ree, kissing her in a way only a lover would.

"My foolish blond lover. You should not have come," Ree whispered into Sylvia's ear. "By doing so you have placed yourself in serious danger. They might arrest you as my co-conspirator."

"A fine role model you make for the young women of

the world," Sylvia giggled. "Ree, my love, you're a stubborn, sarcastic bitch, but you are no murderer. I regret to spoil your martyrdom, but you did not kill Suzuki."

"What the hell are you saying? He is dead. I was there. I watched him die!"

"Most truly the man is dead, but neither you nor I are in any way responsible for it. There is no way I could have allowed you to commit murder. You would only be placing yourself beside him in his coffin had you done it. I was told you attempted to stop the man from finishing his soup. That is proof that you are a good bitch and not an evil bitch."

"I do not understand. Why is Suzuki dead?"

Sylvia looked at Ree with an equally befuddled gaze, shrugging her shoulders. "I cannot say. The poison packet I gave you was actually filled with harmless cornstarch. How and why the man is dead, I cannot answer."

"Dear God, I have eaten myself up with guilt thinking I had poisoned the monster, when all that I really accomplished was to turn his winter melon soup into a stew," Ree mused.

Sylvia's look of puzzlement turned into one of despair. "We have a problem, my love. I have already explained to the authorities that you did not take Suzuki's life. Unfortunately, they think my explanation is merely the act of a woman trying to save her lover's life."

"You were right, my love. I felt no relief or satisfaction when I thought I had killed the monster of my nightmares. You're pretty smart for a lo fon."

Sylvia took Ree's right hand and kissed it. "My beautiful sister, I have as much right to hate the Germans as you do the Japanese. But I made peace with my god. Hating did not return my father to me," she reflected.

Taking the cigarette Sylvia was holding, Ree inhaled a long drag of smoke. "Sylvia, I wish I had some peace." She began to laugh in a rather morose way. "It appears that Suzuki will have the last laugh. He stole my soul years ago, and now he will take my physical life."

Chapter 24

Ree's planned execution was a mere five days away. An autopsy on Hong proved that he did indeed die from the consumption of poison. Having only Sylvia's word, the Chinese government refused to stay Ree's execution, or to even reopen the case.

During the remaining five days, Sylvia visited daily, staying for the fully allotted time. Against regulations, she would sneak Ree her favorite brands of brandy and tequila. During each visit the two old friends and lovers would sit arm in arm, sharing a bottle and memories of better times.

On the fifth day, the hands on the clock appeared to move far more quickly than normal. At 6:00 a.m. sharp Ree would be taken to the courtyard for her execution. At 5:00 a.m. on that last day, Sylvia was allowed to visit her lover one last time. Tears ran heavily down the cheeks of both women. Ree vowed to hold a place in Heaven for Sylvia.

It was 5:55 a.m. when the two women heard the unlocking and opening of the door at the end of the corridor.

"No!" screamed Sylvia at the top of her lungs. "No! We were told 6:00! You have no right to rob me of my last five minutes with Ree! Please, five more minutes. You promised," she begged.

The prison warden and two guards stood before the two women. "Miss Gong, Miss Farnsworth, there has been a slight change in plans. If the two of you will follow us please to the visitors room..."

Confused, the women walked, sandwiched between the guards.

In the room sat an elderly, hunched-over Japanese woman, dressed in a conservative, blue polyester dress. Beside her sat a far younger Japanese woman, sporting a more fashionable yellow dress. Ree and Sylvia gave them a curious look.

"Good morning, Miss Gong, Miss Farnsworth...or should I say Lady Farnsworth?" the younger woman greeted.

"Allow me to introduce to you Fuji Reiko and her granddaughter, Fuji Cherry," said the warden.

"Please, sit with us for a moment," Cherry said to Ree and Sylvia.

Ree and Sylvia complied by sitting at the bare table. The two Japanese women seated themselves across from them.

In a cautious, halted voice, the younger woman began to explain the reason for their visit. "This lady beside me is my grandmother. She is the sister of the Japanese war criminal you know as Suzuki Toro—or Hong Bao, who my uncle was pretending to be. My good grandmother speaks only Japanese, I am here to speak for her."

The young woman pulled a letter from her purse and placed it on the table. It was written in Japanese. "This is a letter from my Granduncle Suzuki to my grandmother. The letter states that he essentially was tired of living. He further states that he recognized you, Miss Gong, as one of his former Nanking victims who he raped and violated. His life had no further purpose, therefore my granduncle took his own life by slipping poison into his wine glass at the memorial dinner."

The revelation was mind-numbing.

"Was he aware that my friend Ree had planned to kill him?" Sylvia asked.

"Not at all. Uncle Suzuki, of course, could have taken his own life in private, but he chose to wait until the day of the memorial so that one of his victims would have the divine pleasure of watching him die. He never forgot your face, or the faces of the countless souls he hurt."

"Did your uncle also burn his face to hide his identity?" Ree inquired.

"Most certainly. But his secondary reason was to make atonement for his sins to you and the countless other Chinese he harmed. Additionally, Hong Bao was one of his victims. The poor man had no living relatives at the time. He was a lowly peasant. Few, if anyone, would miss him. Little did he realize that, to avoid punishment after the war, he had built a prison cell of his own making. He died alone, and no tears were shed by anyone for him. My uncle's wife and son died in the atomic bombing of Hiroshima. It was after this tragedy that Uncle Toro began to understand that the pain he had inflicted on you and your fellow countrymen was wrong. Not to make excuses for my uncle, but it was the brutal treatment of the lower ranking soldiers that turned my uncle and other Japanese soldiers into unprincipled monsters. The harsh, rigid rules of the military hierarchy on the non-officered Japanese soldiers made them take out their misery on the Chinese, or whoever they came in contact with. I know any excuse would seem feeble to you, but it is what it is," explained Cherry.

The old Japanese woman spoke to her granddaughter.

"My grandmother also apologizes to you, Miss Gong, for being so delinquent in coming to Beijing to exonerate you. She is an old, confused woman. She does not always open her letters expediently. She did not open her brother's letter until two days ago, but once she read the letter and learned of your troubles in the newspaper, she contacted me, and together we caught the earliest flight to Beijing. I am also sorry, Miss Gong, for our delay."

Ree and Sylvia breathed a collective sigh of relief.

"Miss Fuji, I am eternally grateful to you and your grandmother for saving my life. Please convey my many thanks to your sweet grandmother in Japanese," Ree said. "But to speak freely, Miss Fuji, I will always hate your granduncle. He was the devil in human form. An infertile turtle egg with no value. The harsh military regime of Japan at that time may have created him and others like him, but we all have choices in life. One cannot justify their acts of evil simply because everyone else made the same choice, or blame their cruelty because a strict military code treated them unfairly," Ree proclaimed.

"Yes, of course," Cherry agreed. "Uncle Suzuki was not a good man during the war years, but in the years after the war he tried very hard to make amends for his sins. Can you not forgive?"

"Sergeant Suzuki Toro tried hard to change, to be a better man. Perhaps he did finally understand my pain and the things he took from me, but I am not yet ready to forgive. For now, I will bury your granduncle, as well. It is time to move on." Ree was now having mixed feelings about the man who had dominated her thoughts the major part of her life.

The four women hugged each other, and the warden officially set Ree free.

"Miss Gong, may you find the peace my granduncle never found," said Cherry as she and her grandmother departed.

Ree and Sylvia walked out of the prison gate, cheered by the protestors who had tried to free her and the omnipresent paparazzi.

"Leave Miss Gong alone, you bloodsucking bastards," cried Sylvia, pushing the aggressive photographers aside.

Borrowing the Beijing mayor's car, they drove the long journey back to Nanking to the place where Ree was born and lived until her teenage years. The rural landscape had changed little over the years.

"Sylvia, I can't stop seeing Suzuki's face before it was disfigured. Why do people like him want to destroy other people's lives? I know what his grandniece said—people that are treated brutally treat others brutally, but is that all there is, my love?"

"Sister, I wish I knew. I suppose Suzuki had a big hole in his soul. I do not think even men like Suzuki know themselves why they kill, rape, and destroy without conscience."

Ree rolled down the window, closed her eyes, and took in a deep breath. "My sister, the country air smells so sweet. I've wanted Suzuki dead by my hand all of my adult life, and now that he's gone, it is time to move on." Ree felt invigorated by the clean air.

Arriving at the former family farm, Ree was delighted to see that the fertile soil was still used to grow her beloved winter melons. They parked the car at the edge of the expansive field. The two women removed their shoes so that they could feel the warm, rich soil under their feet, just as they had when they were young girls.

"The harvest will be good this year," remarked Sylvia, kneeling to inspect one of the ripe melons.

"Stop! You do not belong here!" shouted an elderly man with a wispy beard, walking briskly toward them.

Startled, the two women stood frozen as the man approached.

"Sir, we apologize for trespassing on your property," Sylvia said. "This land once belonged to my girlfriend's family, long ago. We both wanted one last look before returning to America."

"Missy, there is no private land in China. We lease it from the government." The old man squinted his weakened eyes to see the two women more clearly. "Gong Ree? Yes, yes, I remember you as a little girl. I was once a field hand for your father, but only for three seasons. I am Hsu Nee. Please, you and your friend must dine with me and my family. We farm your father's land along with

173

four other families. Feel free to stay as long as you wish."
The old man's excitement grew. "I will a pick a plump
winter melon for our soup. My wife will have dinner
prepared when you are ready to eat." He pointed to a
small house at the edge of the field where Ree's grand
family home once stood. An abrupt look of glee came over
the old man's face. "I have just remembered, your name
was on the radio some days ago. You killed the Butcher
of Nanking. My family also suffered from the hands of
those bastard invaders. You did the world a great service
by killing him." His grin widened. "See you good ladies in
a short while."

Once the old man was out of earshot, the two old
friends burst into outrageous laughter.

"He must not have heard the latest broadcast telling
the world there was a mistake."

"Will you tell the old man the truth—that you were
not Suzuki's executioner?" asked Sylvia.

"Certainly not," Ree replied.

They stood together in the winter melon field,
watching as the sun set, bathing the pale green melons in
a golden yellow.

Sylvia pulled a photo from her coat pocket and
handed it to Ree.

"What a beautiful Italian farmhouse. And a field of
watermelons in the background. What does this photo
represent?" asked Ree.

Sylvia took Ree's right hand. "Beloved sister, it is a
photo of our new home. A hundred acres in California. I
purchased this land four months ago. It was to be a
surprise for your birthday. Who would have guessed you
would have gotten into a little sticky wicket in China?
The Sacramento River borders the east side of the
property. Together we'll tear up the watermelons and
grow your precious winter melons. The Sacramento
valley resembles the good land of your native China."

A few small tears rolled down Ree's face. "We've been

through so much together, my lover and best friend," she reflected.

"I promise you, the best is yet to come," stated Sylvia, as the two of them walked arm in arm to the old farmer's home to dine on winter melon soup.

— THE END —

About the Author

William Wong Foey holds multiple degrees in Fine Art and Social Studies. Mr. Foey taught high school art, and has won numerous awards for creative writing. He has had short stories published in the *Chico News & Review, San Francisco Magazine, Watershed Magazine,* and the *Trans-Pacific Periodical.*

Mr. Foey is of Chinese/American descent, and his family has resided in Red Bluff since the 1850s. He is a frequent speaker on the history of the Chinese in America, including interviews on TV and in periodicals. He is currently a freelance artist and writer.